Bless This Mouse

Bless This Mouse

Lois Lowry

Illustrations by Eric Rohmann

HOUGHTON MIFFLIN HARCOURT
Boston New York

For information about permission to reproduce selections from this book,
write to Permissions, Houghton Mifflin Harcourt Publishing Company,
215 Park Avenue South, New York, New York 10003.

www.hmhco.com

The text of this book is set in Horley Old Style MT.
The illustrations are inkwash and pencil.

The Library of Congress has cataloged the hardcover edition as follows:
Lowry, Lois.
Bless this mouse / written by Lois Lowry and illustrated by Eric Rohmann.
p. cm.
Summary: Mouse Mistress Hildegarde musters all her ingenuity to keep a large
colony of church mice safe from the exterminator and to see that they make it
through the dangerous Blessing of the Animals.
[1. Mice—Fiction.] I. Rohmann, Eric, ill. II. Title.
PZ7.L9673Bl 2011
[Fic]—dc22
2010007331

ISBN: 978-0-547-39009-3 hardcover
ISBN: 978-0-544-43936-8 paperback

Manufactured in the United States of America
DOC 10 9 8 7 6 5 4 3 2 1

4500520117

For
Margaret Holcombe,
so very close to saintly

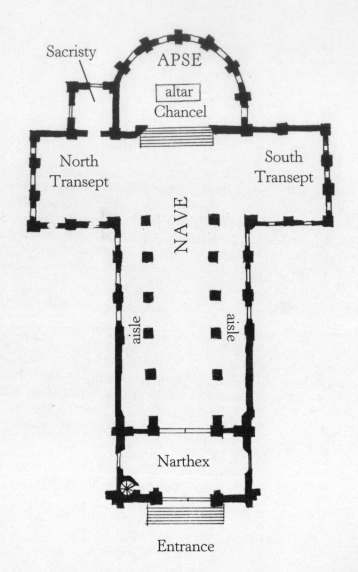

Sacristy

APSE

altar

Chancel

North
Transept

South
Transept

NAVE

aisle

aisle

Narthex

Entrance

Contents

CHAPTER 1

A Bad Time for Babies

Hildegarde sighed, a loud, squeaking, outraged sort of sigh, when she was informed that a new litter of mouselets had been born in the sexton's closet. *Such bad timing! Such bad placement!*

She scurried from the sacristy, the private room where Father Murphy's special priestly clothes were stored. She'd been napping there comfortably, until Roderick, whiskers twitching, woke her with the news. Oh, he was a busybody, no question! Always looking for a reaction. Well, he got one this time! She was furious.

Checking carefully to be certain there were no humans around (sometimes the Altar Guild ladies dropped in during the afternoons to rearrange flowers), Hildegarde tiptoed quickly into the large, high-ceilinged church itself, through the side section known as the transept, and entered the central area called the nave. Audaciously she hurried down the center aisle, ready at any instant to disappear into a pew and under a kneeler if someone entered. But the sanctuary was empty and quiet and she made her way, undisturbed, down its length.

Next she found herself in the narthex. Hildegarde so liked the formal names for the parts of the church. If she were in an ordinary house, she thought, twitching her nose at the idea, this would be known as the front hall. What an *ordinary* name! *Narthex* had a ring to it. You knew you were in an important place when you entered a *narthex!*

There was a tiny opening here, beside the front door, where the floor had settled slightly. Through the opening Hildegarde could enter the wall. The church mice all used this as an entry or exit because stairs were a problem for them. It was easier to ascend or descend inside the wall, where there were tangled wires and frayed insulation to cling to. Carefully, she scurried downward.

Now, having made her way below, she was in the interior wall of the undercroft. Since Hildegarde had lived in Saint Bartholemew's all her life, she knew the route by heart, especially where to scramble over the copper pipes and how to avoid the places where drifting insulation made her sneeze. There were many exits here in the undercroft: one, she recalled, amused as she passed it, into the nursery, a noisy place on Sunday mornings and best avoided. Babies in general were best avoided. They spent time on the floor, could see into crevices, and had graspy hands.

But at least babies couldn't talk, and report a mouse sighting! The group to be most feared, Hildegard thought, was the Altar Guild. More than one of the ladies had actually *shrieked* upon happening on a mouse. Oh, dear. Always an uproar when that happened. (Men seemed to be more sensible about such things.)

Finally, after passing countless Sunday School rooms and making her way carefully around the complicated piping of the bathrooms, Hildegarde arrived at the entrance, a small gnawed hole, to the sexton's closet. She winced when the ragged hole edge grabbed her sleek coat, but wriggled through; then, emerging on the other side within the closet itself, she fastidiously pulled her long, elegant tail through in one swoop.

There they were, curled in a nest made in the sexton's ropey gray mop: at least seven of them, it appeared, and bright pink, a color Hildegarde had always disliked. Annoyed, she looked around. She knew the mother would be nearby. No self-respecting mouse mother would leave infants this young alone. So someone was hiding.

"Show yourself!" Hildegarde commanded. She didn't use her commanding voice terribly often, even though she was the matriarch, the chosen Mouse Mistress, and therefore entitled. But she was angry and nervous. The timing of this was so unfortunate.

The mouse mother responded with a timid squeak, peeping out from between the ropey tangles of a moldy-smelling mop.

"I *knew* it would be you! I just knew it!" Hildegarde said.

"Who told?" squeaked the mouse, guiltily. She made her way over toward the litter, which was beginning to whimper and wiggle at the sound of her voice. She nudged them back into a tidy pile with her nose and then lay down beside the babies, looking up at Hildegarde.

"I simply guessed. It was obvious," Hildegarde said with a sniff. Of course it was Roderick who had told her. "That irresponsible little Millicent has reproduced again," he had announced in his arrogant, judgmental way, after he had poked Hildegarde with his nose and completely ruined her afternoon nap.

She peered down at the young mother. "How many litters does this make?"

Millicent cringed in embarrassment. "Four," she confessed.

"Four this year? Or four overall?" Hildegarde gave an exasperated sniff. "Oh, never mind. It doesn't matter. The point is, as Mouse Mistress, I am commanding you to stop this incessant reproduction! It's jeopardizing all of us. And particularly now. Do you realize it's late September?"

Millicent rearranged herself and the mouselets squirmed against her. "Do you mean it will be cold soon? I can make a nest near a heating duct when the furnace comes on."

"That is not at all what I mean. But you *are* going to have to move this litter someplace else right away. I don't think the sexton's here today. But he'll be in tomorrow, I'm sure. And the instant he reaches for his mop . . ."

Millicent squeaked at the thought.

"Exactly," Hildegarde went on. "Basically, the sexton is fairly tolerant. He'll ignore a few droppings. And I know he overlooked the shredding in his stack of newspapers, though he surely knew it was a nest. That was kind of him. But if he were to encounter . . . *this!*" She gestured toward the pile of pink mouselets. "Well! Do you recall the Great X?"

Millicent cringed. "I've only heard about it," she said nervously.

"No, of course you don't remember. The last Great X was before you were born. But it was simply terrible. We lost half our population! I vowed not to let it happen again. No more haphazard, willy-nilly reproduction! Careful placement! No visibility!" She looked meaningfully at the litter, sleeping now, curled in the stained mop. "We've got to get you and these mouselets moved inside the wall right away."

She considered the problem, then said, "There's

a perfectly good nest left empty after Zachariah's demise." She was silent for a moment, then crossed herself, murmured, "Lord rest his soul," and continued: "It's in the wall behind the men's room toilet. A little noisy, I'm afraid, because of flushing."

"I don't mind flushing," Millicent squeaked.

"Let's get started, then. If you take one and I take another, we can get them all moved in three or four trips." Hildegarde leaned down and took a deep breath. "Oh," she muttered, "this is not pleasant at all." Then she grasped a mouselet by its neck and moved back through the hole into the wall, carrying it carefully, its miniature legs and tail dangling in a slightly wiggly way.

Preparing to come after her, Millicent paused and said in a sulky voice, "Lucretia thinks they're cute."

Hildegarde heard her but didn't dignify the comment with a response. She couldn't stand Lucretia, who had competed against her for the role of Mouse Mistress using unfair tactics, and had been a very poor sport about losing.

She continued on, carrying the mouselet. But now she was even more furious. *Lucretia!* Her rival. Her worst enemy. And a *liar,* too. *Cute?* These mouselets were a hideous shade of pink, and their ribs showed. They were not cute at all.

CHAPTER 2

Praying for Protection

It wasn't simply a problem of placement and visibility. Those things were important, of course, because it was vital that the mouse population remain unseen, and now that she and Millicent had succeeded in moving the mouselets, Hildegarde gave a relieved sigh. Now, at least, the sexton would not open the closet door, gasp, and rush to a telephone to arrange for another Great X.

But it was the timing, too. Late September. They were approaching such a dangerous moment.

"Are *you*, at least, aware of the time of year?" she

asked Roderick. "Millicent was completely oblivious." They were in the chancel, seated together at the base of the lectern, dining together on a selection of crumbs and a smear of apricot jam, all of it salvaged from the kitchen wastebasket.

Roderick delicately cleaned one whisker with a paw. He sucked some jam from one of his big front teeth. He and Hildegarde chose different dining places each day, and although the base of the lectern was a favorite—it was pleasant to lean back against the polished wood—it had the disadvantage of no napkins. When they dined in the sacristy, with all of its stored vestments, there was always an alb or a stole handy for wiping one's mouth and whiskers. He tidied himself as best he could without a napkin. Then he said, echoing Hildegarde, "The time of year."

(Roderick didn't have any idea what she was talking about. But he had found that sometimes, to avoid sounding stupid, it was wise simply to repeat.)

She nibbled her final crumb, and said meaningfully, "The church calendar."

"Yes," Roderick repeated. "The church calendar."

"The Feast of Saint Francis," Hildegarde said meaningfully.

"Of course." Roderick licked a little jam from his paw. "I do love the word *feast*, don't you?"

"Roderick! You do remember Saint Francis, of course? Look *up*, would you?"

Oh, dear. Hildegarde was using her extremely exasperated voice. And she was *pointing*. He tried very hard to recall what she meant. He looked up. Oh, yes. Stained-glass windows. Saints.

He chose one at random, gazed at it ruefully, and hoped he was correct. "Arrows in the stomach! Dreadful. Absolutely dreadful."

She gave him a withering look. "That's Saint Sebastian."

"I knew that," he said hastily. He looked around. There were numerous windows depicting people in

pain of various kinds. But he followed Hildegarde's pointing paw, and suddenly there he was—how could Roderick have forgotten?—Saint Francis, the one smiling, with a bird on his shoulder and another eating from his outstretched hand.

"Dear Saint Francis," Roderick said reverently.

"Lover of animals," Hildegarde murmured, gazing at the window where the saint, in his simple brown robe, was depicted in translucent shades of colored glass. Then she shook herself. "Anyway, his feast day is October fourth. You surely knew that."

Roderick smiled politely, hiding his ignorance.

"It's a terribly dangerous time for us. We've had some very narrow escapes on October fourths in the past," she reminded him. "Especially if it rains."

"Indeed. Very narrow."

"Oh, Roderick, you old fool. You don't have any idea what I'm talking about! And," she added, "you have jam on one whisker. Tidy yourself, please, at once."

He did so, and then held his head for her inspection. He so hoped Hildegarde would find him, well, attractive.

But she simply nodded in approval that the jam had been removed. "It's the Blessing of the Animals," she explained impatiently.

Roderick gulped. *Now* he remembered. How could one forget such a frightening event? "Oh my goodness," he said with a shudder. "Cats."

"Exactly. We must pray."

"Now?"

"Now wouldn't hurt. It's probably a good idea to start well in advance."

Roderick nodded, brushed a crumb from his belly fur, bowed his head, and cleared his throat. "Heavenly Father," he began in as humble a tone as possible, "this is a church mouse speaking. We are understandably fearful of cats."

Hildegarde, beside him, murmured her own version, and together they explained the dangerous situation coming up and asked for heightened security and a day with bright sunshine. "If it be Thy will," Hildegarde added politely at the conclusion.

"Yes, of course," Roderick said. "Amen."

The Blessing of the Animals took place every year at Saint Bartholemew's—outdoors, in the churchyard garden, if the weather was good, and fortunately it had been, for several years now. Rain? The whole thing moved inside. For the church mice, a rainy October fourth was much to be feared.

The ceremony was held in honor of the twelfth-century monk Francis of Assisi. Saint Francis had, it was said, so loved all living creatures that he had preached to the birds and they had silenced their twittering, sat very still on their branches, and listened attentively. The stained-glass window indicated that they had sat on his shoulders and in the palm of his outstretched hand, as well, though there is no way to know, after more than eight hundred years, whether that was true.

Each year the parishioners were invited to bring their pets to be blessed. Each year the ceremony had become larger and larger in numbers, and the previous year, the procession had wound out of the churchyard and down the small road that led to the church.

The church newsletter had requested that pet owners, when appropriate, bring scoopers and plastic bags. Golden retrievers, especially, overwhelmed by the magnificence and solemnity, often let loose on the flagstone path.

Cleanup wasn't necessary, of course, for turtles or canaries, and there were always several of both. Children carried cages and terrariums. Dogs walked beside their owners on leashes. Toddlers clutched pet bunnies. Last year a young girl had brought her horse, its bridle entwined with fall asters and ribbons. Walking beside its owner, the horse suddenly paused and peed what seemed to be gallons onto a ground-cover of periwinkle. Everyone in the procession waited politely, because there is no way to interrupt a horse mid-pee. The priest, Father Murphy, a passionate gardener, closed his eyes during the wait, and many people suspected he was praying for the survival of his periwinkle. Nonetheless, when the horse, who was by then loudly munching a bouquet of late daylilies that he had wrenched from a decorative border, reached the front of the line, the good father smiled benignly, touched the coarse mane with a few drops of holy oil, and bestowed a blessing.

Hildegarde, recalling this, could imagine the loud clop of horse hooves on the tiled center aisle had the day been rainy last year. But the sun had been brightly shining on the October morning. She and other church mice had watched the event, as they always did, from inside the sanctuary, through peepholes and windows. Several brave adolescents had made their way up into the belfry, and later described the view of the procession from such a high place. The horse, they reported, seemed as small as a mouse; a Saint Bernard was minuscule as they looked down on him; and the cats the many, many cats—were barely visible, just pieces of fluff in children's arms.

Video cameras always whirred in the background, and in recent years the local TV station had sent a cameraman and a reporter, who whispered into a microphone as if she were commenting on a golf tournament. Two years ago the perky reporter, eyes widening in amazement as a large, stately animal led by a woman holding its halter strode past, had murmured into the mike, "My goodness! I believe this is a llama we're seeing!" But the creature's owner, overhearing the reporter, turned with a frown and corrected her tersely. "Vicuña," she said.

It was a memorable, impressive event every October. But Hildegarde and Roderick, praying now for divine protection as the time of the ceremony approached, understood exactly what danger was facing them at the Blessing of the Animals.

The procession and ceremony grew bigger and more disorganized every year.

If it happened to rain, it all moved inside.

Inside was where the population of church mice lived.

And there were always, always cats.

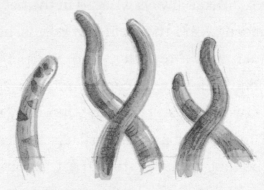

CHAPTER 3

Hildegarde Holds a Meeting

Church mice had inhabited Saint Bartholemew's for generations. Occasionally, during a Great X (the thing they feared most, even more than they feared cats) their numbers would be decimated, for a Great X was a hideous thing and cost many lives. But with their capacity—the same capacity that Hildegarde was trying now to curtail—for what she called "incessant reproduction," they always fought back and increased their population once again.

Hildegarde was not wrong to try to limit the numbers. Too many church mice was a very dangerous situation.

Many humans came and went at Saint Bartholemew's: Father Murphy, of course; Miss Vickery, the church secretary; the Altar Guild ladies; Trevor Fisoli, the organist/choirmaster, and his award-winning men-and-boys choir; Alcoholics Anonymous members, who met on Thursday evenings; the sexton; the scoutmaster and his scouts; the visiting bishop; and countless others. Occasionally someone glanced down, saw a mouse, and said something such as "Yikes" or even "Eek." (Or, if it was an Altar Guild lady, particularly Ruth Ellen van Riper, "Oh my GAWD!")

But that would be the end of it. Perhaps the person would say, "There's a mouse in the church." But by then the visible mouse had scampered away and become invisible. People shrugged, chuckled, and forgot.

Ironically, they all thought they were seeing the *same mouse.*

It was Hildegarde, actually, who realized that they were making that mistake. She attended an Alcoholics Anonymous meeting on a Thursday night in late September, hidden, of course—in fact, quite concealed behind a potted plant in the corner of the room.

She liked AA meetings because they served cookies and always had a lot of leftovers.

Waiting for them to adjourn so that she could collect their leavings, Hildegarde drowsed a bit (their meetings were very boring, she thought). Then, suddenly, she heard the word "mouse." So she sat upright and listened.

Later she called a meeting of the church mice (just before dawn on Saturday, a time when the building was certain to be empty of humans). They streamed, more than two hundred of them, into Father Murphy's private office. They liked holding their meetings there because of the many bookshelves. Carefully they arranged themselves in rows, each mouse seated in front of the spine of a leatherbound book. Sometimes one of them, overwhelmed by temptation, nibbled at the leather, though there was an unwritten rule against that.

(But never Bibles. The church mice never nibbled Bibles. It would have been unthinkable.)

Hildegarde stood on Father Murphy's desk, next to his calendar (on which she noted *BLESSING OF*

ANIMALS written in red ink and coming up very, very soon) and watched as the population arranged itself.

"Harvey!" she called to a young mouse who was frequently inattentive. "Stop that right now! Don't make a mess of that!"

Harvey twitched his tail and made a face. He was perched on the coffee table in front of Father Murphy's couch, and he'd been poking with interest at an arrangement of playing cards that was laid out there in an unfinished game of solitaire. Sometimes,

in the late afternoon, Father Murphy amused himself that way.

Roderick, on the desk near her, saw a way to impress Hidegarde with his intelligence. He whispered, "The red three could go on the black four."

Hildegarde gave him an exasperated look. Then she tapped for silence, using a pencil against the telephone. "The reason I've assembled you," Hildegarde began when they were all comfortably arranged and quiet, "is because Thursday evening I dropped in on an AA meeting—"

"Oooohh!" squealed a young female named Desirée. "Cookie crumbs, cookie crumbs, cookie crumbs!"

Hildegarde glared at her until she contained herself.

"—and I overheard someone, a woman, say that she had seen a mouse in the ladies' room."

She looked around the office. "This would have been Thursday, about seven p.m.," she reminded them.

"Anyone?" she asked, meaningfully.

No one stirred for a moment. Then, finally, obviously embarrassed, a middle-aged female named Norma raised her paw. "That would have been me. Sorry. I went through the ladies' room because it was a shortcut. I hate making my way around the wiring in that wall."

"Yes, the wiring there is awful. One of us is going to be electrocuted someday," another mouse called from his high perch on a shelf where *The Lives of the Philosophers* were stored.

"I knew there was a meeting going on but I thought AA was all men," Norma explained. "I thought the ladies' room was safe."

"Oh my, no," Hildegarde said. "Half women. Including the church secretary."

"So I was wrong, obviously. And there I was, in the middle of the room, when a woman came in. I scampered away, but I know she saw me. I'm sorry. Is it a disaster? Will it bring on the Great X?"

Norma wrung her tiny paws nervously.

A low, frightened murmur made its way around the room.

"Not by itself. But hear me out," said Hildegarde. "The next day, Friday—that would be yesterday—I was in the sacristy, about to take my afternoon nap—"

"She always naps in the sacristy," Roderick interrupted loudly, hoping that all the mice would notice what a close and special relationship he had with Hildegarde. She glared at him. He looked the other way and fell silent.

She continued, "—when I overheard the sexton talking to that woman who heads up the Altar Guild. The woman with the ugly hat?"

The church mice nodded their heads and murmured. They all knew the hat. "She's the one who says 'Eek,'" someone said, and they all giggled.

"Well," Hildegarde went on, "the sexton was teasing her a little, I think. He told her to watch out if she took that hat off and set it down, because it looked like a good nest for mice, and he'd seen a mouse—"

"It *would* be a great nest!" squeaked a youngster who'd been perched on the arm of the deep red sofa. "If she ever puts it in the rummage bin, we should grab it!"

Hildegarde glared again. She hated interruptions. When they were silent, she continued. "He told her he'd seen a mouse that morning in the kitchen, under the sink."

"Oh dear, oh dear. That was me." A large male mouse stood up on his back legs, raised one front paw, and continued his confession. "I came up beside the water pipe. I was going to grab part of an SOS pad and take it back to my nest. I like a little firmness to my bed. But just as I got there, someone opened the cabinet door and reached in for a sponge. So I took off. I didn't realize he'd seen me.

"I'm so, so sorry. Does it mean the Great X? Please, no!"

"Shhh. Let me finish. I heard the sexton describe that sighting to the Bad Hat Lady, and he said, 'We seem to have a mousie in the church. Someone saw it last night in the ladies' room.'"

"A *mousie?*" Dozens of them repeated the word, tittering.

"Shhh!" Hildegarde admonished them sternly. "Finally, last night, as he was leaving for the rectory, Father Murphy said to the sexton, 'That mouse really gets around. I saw him scoot across the hall when I went to the men's room!'"

"Him? *Him?*" Millicent sounded outraged. "Does that man not recognize a nursing mother when he sees one? I was hurrying home to the mouselets. All right, I shouldn't have crossed the hall in broad daylight, I know that—"

"*Hush*," Hildegarde said. "I am simply pointing out a very fortunate thing. Three different people—

the AA lady, the sexton, and Father Murphy—saw three different mice—"

"Me," the three guilty mice said in guilty unison.

"—but they all think they saw the same mouse! They think Saint Bartholemew's has *one mouse!*"

"Instead of *hundreds!*" Roderick called out gleefully. Around the room, from their various perches on shelves and sofas and table, two hundred and eighteen (one had not attended; he was old, and sleeping) church mice applauded with their little paws. Mouse paws are softly padded, so applause is a muted, muffled sound. But the congratulatory clapping together of several hundred paws does make a distinctive noise. Hildegarde allowed them their moment of jubilation before she called for quiet.

From the corner of Father Murphy's office, a tall clock chimed four. It was still dark, pre-dawn. Roderick yawned.

"I'll let you go now," Hildegarde said. "But I want you to understand that we must maintain this illusion. We must be as *one mouse.* We must not be revealed as the multitude that we are.

"Keep yourselves hidden!" she instructed them as they clambered down from the shelves and prepared to leave. "At all times! Otherwise . . ."

They knew how to fill in the blank. "The Great X," they murmured ominously as they spread out and began to scamper in great numbers down the halls and aisles and passages of the church.

"And all of you?" Hildegarde called after them. "Please! Pray for sun on October fourth!"

"*Pray for sun on October fourth!*" A sarcastic voice mimicked her. Hildegarde turned and saw her enemy, the mouse she most loathed. Lucretia, sneering casually, turned and strolled down the aisle, her wide rump swaying.

CHAPTER 4

Hiding from Father Murphy

The life of a mouse can for the most part be described in verbs. *Arrive. Grow. Forage. Eat. Sleep. Mate. Reproduce. Age. Die.*

Of course, each of those verbs has subcategories. Foraging, for example, involves scampering, searching, finding, opening, nibbling, stealing, hiding, escaping, and countless other verbs involved in the nightly act of food gathering.

It is the same for all kinds of mice. The tiny pygmy mouse forages, eats, grows, mates, reproduces, and ages in the same way that the grasshopper mouse, the striped field mouse, the African climbing mouse, and the South American leaf-eared mouse do.

But a church mouse has a more complicated life.

Oh, there was so very much to tend to! It was Sunday, and Sundays were especially busy times. Hildegarde rose from her night nest behind the expression pedal of the pipe organ. She always rose very early, particularly on Sundays, when the organist arrived to practice well before anyone else had entered the church. Sometimes Hildegarde scurried away just as he came up the stairs to the choir loft. But she had never been seen, and he had never noticed her small nest there, just behind the pedal where he placed his foot when he wanted a dramatic increase in volume. Sometimes the expression pedal was called the "swell pedal" because it caused the music to swell gloriously. But Hildegarde thought that a rather vulgar term.

It was still dawn. She tidied her nest, making sure it would be invisible; then from the loft she entered the wall and descended past the main floor and down into the undercroft, where she turned right and made her way through the maze of wires and pipes, stopping here and there to check on the population. Good. They were all deeply concealed and well provided with food. Nighttime was foraging time, and after the church was darkened and silent, they had emerged, all of them, spreading out to check all the potential nourishment sources. The supply closet of the nursery was a great resource, for it contained paste, and usually the lid of the large paste jar was not tightly closed. The tips of crayons were tasty to some, though Hildegarde did not care much herself for their waxy flavor. There were always cookie crumbs in the nursery carpeting. She let the young mice have those because they enjoyed the game of it, vying with each other as they looked for morsels. Hildegarde had seen human children play the same game at Easter time. searching for jellybeans.

(And oh! The jellybeans they missed! Hildegarde particularly loved the black ones.)

The kitchen, of course, was the best location. The church ladies prided themselves on their tidiness, but if they only knew! The wastebaskets! Paper plates with sticky crumbs still attached! Packets of Splenda still half full! And in the cupboards: boxes, not tightly closed (and did it matter, really? For they could gnaw! Oh, they were excellent at gnawing!), of flour and sugar and pasta of all sorts. Father Murphy's office had a hidden cache of chocolates and gumdrops (he was supposed to be dieting), pipe tobacco (not too yummy, but some mice liked just a smidgeon occasionally), and now and then homemade cookies, which his mother sent him from Ohio. Plus, after Christmas, there were *so many* fruitcakes!

And flowers. There were flowers everywhere, in every season, and the time after weddings and funerals were particularly bountiful, though the young mice had to be reminded often that hollyberries

and poinsettia leaves were poisonous. So tempting, the bright reds! But every year, despite the warnings, there was a mishap, and a sad ending for an unfortunate mouse who didn't heed the wisdom of elders.

Daylilies were delicious. And candles—there were many candles available—were filling, though not too tasty.

Hildegarde continued on, checking everyone. Millicent's babies were up and about now, with fur and wide eyes. "Keep them close and out of sight," she reminded Millicent sternly. "They haven't developed any sense yet." Millicent made a squeaky sound of assent and gathered her rambunctious mouselets, anchoring one with her paw on its tail.

Making the rounds, Hildegarde chuckled, noticing two brand-new traps baited with cheese: one in the ladies' room, one under the kitchen sink. The sexton was trying to catch the "one mouse" that had been seen. Using a thick straw wrenched from the sexton's broom, she nudged the cheese, springing the traps, and then called two of the brawnier mice to cart the cheddar pieces away and divvy them up quickly before the church day began.

Next, she made her way to the sacristy, her favorite place because of its beautiful priestly vestments: the crisp white surplices, the mossy greens and royal purples of the various robes, the narrow stoles with colorful embroidery, and the cincture, a kind of sash woven with gold thread. Hildegarde looked around, making certain everything was in place. This was her traditional afternoon napping place and she did not allow the other church mice here; young ones, especially, would have been too tempted to nibble on the array of magnificent borders and threads. It is a tendency of mice to pull and fray fabric; they mean no harm but are always looking for ways to enhance their nests. She had noticed, actually, that Millicent had woven some deep red threads into the nest of torn paper towels where she was raising her mouselets. Hildegarde suspected, recognizing the color, that the deep red had been pulled from a pew cushion. Many of the mice had used such a red, she knew, and if it was not overdone . . . well, it could be overlooked. Church mice deserved some beauty in their lives. And a pew cushion . . . well, there were rows and rows of them. Hildegarde had no particular feelings for pew cushions.

The sacristy, though? Absolutely forbidden. It was sacrosanct.

Hildegarde, older and self-disciplined, simply tidied things for Father Murphy. If a thread had been loosened from the hem of a vestment sleeve, she nibbled it carefully to neaten the border. If a surplice was poorly folded, she nudged it into a more orderly alignment. This morning, twitching her small nose, she looked around. Sunday mornings were the crucial ones. But today things seemed in order. She would check later, after the service, for crumbs. Though Father Murphy was very meticulous, the altar boys were careless—more than careless: sometimes actually malicious!—and there were occasionally tiny bits of communion wafers dropped. Once a Life Saver! Hildegarde always ate everything very reverently, even the Life Saver, which had been fuzzy with pocket lint and completely unappetizing.

WHOOOOOMMM! Hildegarde jumped. Trevor Fisoli had arrived and was testing the organ up in the loft. He was using the crescendo pedal, and starting with the loudest possible chord at full throttle. All right, *throttle* wasn't the right word. She knew that. But Hildegarde felt that the crescendo pedal was very much like the gas pedal of a car. (And yes, Hildegarde had been in a car. She had found herself trapped in a child's backpack once, when she'd been looking for cookies during Sunday School. It was a foolish mistake; she was embarrassed, remembering. It took her a week to make her way back to Saint Bartholemew's.)

She pictured Trevor as the driver—sometimes like a little old lady hunched behind the wheel, going very cautiously, other times revving up like a racecar driver at the track. He always started his private rehearsal with that full-out sound. It was what kept her night nest, there under his right foot (if he only knew!), nicely flattened and firm.

Next he segued into a Bach fugue. Although she couldn't see him from the sacristy, Hildegarde pictured Trevor (often she had watched him from a hiding place behind a chair leg in the alto section), his fingers flying, his hair flying, too, as he moved his head rapturously. He should get his hair cut short, she thought. Mice were fortunate. Their fur grew, gray and sleek, to exactly the length that suited them. But humans! Well! They were left to their own devices and seemed to have no sense of the appropriate. Trevor's hair was shoulder-length and he didn't comb it often enough. Father Murphy's was short (and gray, which was pleasantly familiar), and he combed it frequently but oddly, to try to cover the balding top of his head.

The sound of the organ reminded her that she

must hurry. Soon the choir members would arrive. Father Murphy would be donning his vestments and preparing the sacraments. Oops! There he was now, entering. She darted under the edge of the draperies and hid. She could see, peeking under the edge of the thick velvet (which was slightly frayed—she should nibble those borders and clean up that edge a bit), his black shoes on the dark blue carpet. The shoes walked around the room.

Then she could hear him calling to the sexton in the hall.

"Were you in the sacristy last night? I left something in here that seems to have disappeared."

"Nope. I vacuumed in there Thursday. Haven't been in since."

"Well, that's a mystery!" Fortunately Father Murphy's tone was mildly amused. Hildegarde cringed. He must be talking about the chocolate-covered cherry left beside the sink. She'd assumed he had dropped it and didn't know. Never dreamed he'd go looking for it! It wasn't even that good. Much too sweet and sticky. Now she was sorry she'd eaten it.

She waited, very quiet, while he made his preparations and donned his vestments for the service. In the distance she could hear people entering and taking seats in the pews. Usually, by now, Hildegarde was inside the wall and completely invisible. She shouldn't have dallied in the kitchen and ladies' room, but of course the cheese was a great find. As soon as Father Murphy left the sacristy to join the altar boys and crucifer and choir lining up in the narthex for the processional hymn, she'd make her escape and take up her Sunday morning duties with her own population. There! He was going now. She took advantage of the moment as the door closed behind him. She scampered across the carpet and entered the wall where there was an opening for the pipes to the sacristy sink.

She cleared her throat and murmured the words under her breath, preparing. *"We have followed too much the devices and desires of our own hearts,"* she murmured. Down the wiring she scrambled, leveling off on the floor below. She scurried along toward the furnace room, murmuring still. The echo was nice here, she thought. *"We have left undone those things which we ought to have done and we have done those things which we ought not to have done . . ."* Okay. She was in good voice now.

Hastily she scurried to the spot where, perched on the furnace oil tank (somehow there was a good reverberation there), she could best be heard by her own congregation.

No human knew this, of course. But each week Hildegarde led all the church mice in confession. And they sang.

CHAPTER 5

A Nighttime Raid

Father Murphy had, as usual, spilled a little wine in the sacristy. Hildegarde didn't touch the stuff herself, but Roderick liked a nip now and then. She summoned him after things were closed up and the church was empty. Then she watched while he cleaned the counter, licking the wine tidily. She had just overheard very bad news, and he would be the first to know about it.

"There," Roderick said. He sat up, balancing himself with his tail, and looked around. He hiccuped. It didn't take much wine to make Roderick a little tipsy. "Any more?" he asked hopefully. "Sometimes he dribbles some on the floor. I could get it before it soaks in."

They both peered down and examined the carpet from where they were perched. "Just old stains," Hildegarde said. "Nothing worth licking."

"I guess not." Roderick looked a little dejected. He always hoped for a major spill. But Father Murphy was pretty careful with the wine. "Well, I think we're finished up in here, then." He giggled a little. "Thank you, Hilly. You're a dear."

She glared at him—she hated being called by that nickname—but he didn't notice. "Time for a nap!" he announced, with another small hiccup.

"Wait. I have news."

"News?" Roderick hopped down to a low shelf. "Don't tell me Millicent's expecting again. Puh-leeze!"

"No, no, it's not that." Hildegarde jumped down and sat beside him on the shelf. She noticed a satin ribbon extending from the edge of a prayer book. Satin was tasty, and she was tempted. But she let it go. "We've been so vigilant about Millicent's babies," she said, "that I fear we have not been sufficiently attentive to some others."

"Others?" Roderick asked.

"Vivian's litter," Hildegarde said.

"*Them?* Awful bunch. Poorly behaved." Roderick gave an exasperated snort.

"Indeed. And Vivian allowed them to run loose. All around the sanctuary. They played hide-and-seek among the kneelers. She said they'd been cooped up and needed some exercise."

"When?"

"Just before the service. I was in the kitchen at the time."

"Were they seen?"

Hildegarde nodded. "The entire Altar Guild."

"Oh, no! Was there shrieking? And *eek*s?"

"Apparently. I didn't hear it. Others did. I was dealing with the traps, getting the cheese extricated."

"Oh, and thank you for that, dear," Roderick said. "It was a lovely Vermont cheddar."

"Yes, I know. I had a taste. At any rate, the Altar Guild saw several of Vivian's offspring—"

Roderick made a *tsk-tsk* sound. "She should have better control of them."

"Well, of course she should. But they're five weeks old, Roderick. You know what that means."

"Oh, lord. Adolescents. No controlling them." Roderick rolled his eyes.

"I told her to give them a lecture this morning after confession. Explain to them what '*We have done those things which we ought not to have done*' means."

"They won't listen. Adolescents never listen."

"I fear the consequences," Hildegarde said ominously. "They know now that we are more than one."

"You really think? Consequences?" Roderick had become drowsy because of the wine. But now his eyes widened. "Oh, no! A Great X?"

"A Great X," Hildegarde repeated. "I heard Father Murphy talking to the sexton before they closed up the church. They used the *X* word. We must try to find a way to stop it."

They sat together, thinking. Finally, Roderick said, "I have a plan."

"A plan?"

"I know you think I am just a doddering fool. I know you have little respect for my intelligence, Hildegarde. I know you become impatient when I go on and on—"

"As you are doing at this moment," she pointed out, glaring. "What is your plan, exactly, Roderick?"

He drew himself up as if to make a pronouncement. "We must go in to Father Murphy's office," he said, "before it's too late . . ."

"Too late for what?"

"Before he has called in the Great X."

"Well, today is Sunday. He's at the rectory having a pot roast dinner. Then he'll read the *New York Times*, watch football, and take a nap. Tonight he'll watch *Masterpiece Theatre*. He won't do anything meaningful until tomorrow," Hildegarde said.

"We must do it now, then."

"Do *what*, Roderick?"

Roderick took a deep breath. "It won't be easy," he said.

"*What* won't?"

Roderick hiccuped again, excused himself politely,

then said in a determined voice, "We must eat his telephone book."

⌇

It was certainly not going to be easy. Hildegarde and Roderick quickly gathered a group of stealthy, strong helpers. Frederick and Marvin were well known for having once gnawed through the base of the pantry door. They made an opening small enough that it went unnoticed by the humans, but large enough that during the night several regiments of mice entered and removed a great many peanut butter crackers that had been stored there for use on a Sunday School hiking trip.

Jeremiah was famous in the church mouse community for having chewed access, once, through the base of a heavy polyurethane trash can at a time when a Youth Group pizza get-together had deposited many leftover crusts still daubed with cheese—quite a find.

There were twelve of them altogether, most selected on the basis of their proven chewing ability, and a few, such as Norma and Charles, picked because of tidying skills. It was important not to leave any evidence, and so some mice had been chosen to be the cleanup squad.

Now, knowing that Father Murphy, next door at the rectory, was watching a football game on television and drinking a beer, which would make him very sleepy very soon, the team of mice, all twelve, gathered in the narthex. The church was empty and silent. There was no need to sneak, for a change. So, boldly, they marched, two by two, led by Hildegarde and Roderick, down the center aisle, singing "Onward Christian Soldiers" as loudly as their squeaky little voices could manage.

Then, after they had turned right at the chancel and passed through the south transept into a hallway, they stopped singing. At the end of the hall they entered Father Murphy's office silently, in single file. The room was tidy, with everything neatly arranged. His cache of candy was well hidden, and the solitaire game was gone from the table, the playing cards neatly in their box. Magazines were stacked and the newspaper was folded.

Good. Hildegarde had worried that it might be in a drawer, but the thick telephone book was right there on his desk.

"It's huge," squeaked Frederick.

"Humungous," Jeremiah agreed, "and it won't even taste good."

One by one, Hildegarde leading the way, they jumped first onto Father Murphy's chair and then to the desktop. They surrounded the thick book, eyeing it with apprehension. "I have a thought," Hildegarde said suddenly.

They waited, listening.

"If we could open it . . ." she began.

"I think we can!" Marvin said. Marvin was the strongest of all the mice. He moved forward and put his front paws on the side of the book. He riffled the edges of the pages. "If we all push at once, it will open, I think."

"Well," Hildegarde explained, "if we can push it open to the Xs—"

"Brilliant!" interrupted Roderick. "Why bother eating the As or Bs or Cs? We just need to find—"

"THE GREAT X!" the mice shouted in unison.

They lined up along the edge of the book. "Count of three," Frederick said. "One, two . . ."

"Three!" Everyone shouted squeakily, and pushed. The thick book opened slightly at the middle.

"Hop inside and keep pushing!" Frederick directed. Huffing and puffing, the mice scrambled up the side and into the opening. "I'm too old for this," Hildegarde complained. But she held her own.

"Now push!" Frederick commanded. "Really, really hard!"

Grunting with the effort, they all pushed and the book opened wider. "Don't let go, or we'll be squashed!" called Jeremiah. Determinedly they pushed and pushed, and finally the book fell completely open on the desk.

"Whew!" Hildegarde fell back in exhaustion. Around her, the eleven others all collapsed on the open pages, panting but triumphant.

"Uh-oh," Roderick muttered, looking down. "We opened to the *P*s."

"How far is that from *X*?" asked Norma. "I can never remember the alphabet."

"Quite a distance, I'm afraid," Hildegarde said. She stood up. "But from here it's easier. We'll just turn a few pages at a time until we get to *X*. Look!" She lifted a page with her paw and they could see how light it was. But there were such a lot of them!

"Or we could eat them," Marvin suggested. He took a small bite of a *P* page, and made a face. "It tastes awful," he said.

"Hey!" Frederick shouted. "Look!" He aimed his tail carefully and flipped a page open with it. "We can do it with our tails! Are all of your tails in good shape?"

There were squeaks and nods.

"All right then. Line up."

It took them a little while to get the hang of it. But after a bit of practice, and with Hildegarde calling directions (her own tail was a little weak, having once been caught in a door), the mice began turning the pages quite rapidly by using their tails as tools.

"*Q!*"

"*R!*"

"*S!*"

They made their way through the alphabetized pages until finally they arrived at *X*. There they stopped to rest.

"My tail is tired," Charles said.

"Mine too," echoed several other mice.

"When we get back, we'll go to the hot water pipe by the men's room and drape our tails over it for a while," Hildegarde said. "A little heat treatment will fix us right up."

She jumped up on the open page. "You know, we don't even really need to eat all the X pages. We just need to find the Great X and destroy that page. If we do it carefully, and then close the book again—"

The other mice all groaned. Closing the book would mean another huge pushing effort.

"Well, maybe we could leave it open. He'll probably think he left it that way. We'll just have to nibble the edges so carefully that he won't notice the missing page."

"Norma and I will tidy it up," Charles said. "We're very, very good at that."

"All right," Hildegarde announced. "Let's find the Great X." She looked down at the page she was standing on and read: "X-Treme Bodybuilding."

"Nope," Frederick said. "That's not it."

"X-rated DVDs."

"Nope."

"X-ercise Bikes."

"Nope."

"X-cellent Cake Decorating."

"Nope."

Hildegarde read on and on through the three full pages of Xs.

But the Great X was simply not there.

Dejectedly the mice decided that it would serve no purpose to eat the entire telephone book. To make themselves bloated and sick, and for what?

They gave up. One by one they lowered themselves from the desk. Tails drooping, they left the office and trudged down the hall, through the transept, across the front of the chancel, and back down the center aisle, heads bowed in disappointment.

Lucretia appeared, waddling across the narthex. She stared at them contemptuously. "Problems?" she asked, with a malicious smile. Lucretia was always hoping for some way to oust Hildegarde and elevate herself to the position of Mouse Mistress. "Something you can't solve, Hildegarde? Getting a little old? Need my help?"

She smirked.

"No," Hildegarde replied tersely, and continued on past.

The line of dejected mice entered the wall one by one. It was rather like a funeral, Hildegarde thought, as she brought up the end of the slow, sad procession. But at least at a funeral, there were flowers to eat.

CHAPTER 6

The Great X

Father Murphy made the call first thing Monday morning. Hildegarde was watching from behind the radiator. She had taken the shortcut through the wall to his office and emerged beside the radiator pipe. It was a route that was too dangerous in winter, when the pipes were hot. But now, at the end of September, the furnace had not yet been turned on.

She saw him turn the pages of the telephone book and then run his finger down the page until he found the number. Amazingly, it was near the *front* of the book, not the back, where they had found the *X* pages.

Hildegarde was puzzled by that. She hoped he would leave the book open so that later, when he had left the room, she could check. Perhaps all by herself she could eat that page, in case there was a next time. But for now, it was too late. Father Murphy picked up the receiver and dialed. At the same time, he called to the church secretary, who was in the small room nearby.

"I'm making arrangements to have the rodent problem taken care of, Sylvia," he told her.

Hildegarde shuddered. To be lumped like that into the category of *rodent!* Awful! That category included *rats,* a terrible enemy of mice! She knew that technically church mice were rodents. But to have it said so blatantly! Well. *Well!*

She waited, listening to his conversation, then watched while he hung up the phone, rose from his desk, sneaked a couple of gumdrops from their hiding place into his mouth, and left the room. "He'll be here Wednesday," she heard him tell the secretary.

Quickly she scampered over to his desk and examined the opened telephone book. Too late for this time. The church mice would have to deal with Wednesday and what it would bring. But next time—if there was ever a next time—they'd be better prepared.

The page was in the *E*s. And there it was: a little boxed ad, with silhouettes of mice displayed (not very well drawn, she observed; the ears were too small, and the noses overly pointed, giving the silhouettes an evil appearance). And she could see immediately the mistake they had made. The person Father Murphy had called was actually the EXTERMINATOR.

So it was *EX*, not *X*. Well! Live and learn!

And Hildegarde had an *EX* of her own now to plan, she realized—a special kind of *EX* she had learned about from listening to readings from the Bible. She had saved this word for the moment it was needed, a moment she had hoped would never come.

She grabbed a gumdrop—a green one, her favorite flavor; no sense wasting the opportunity!— and scurried back across the

room and down into the radiator pipe opening. When she reached the undercroft, she went first to her secret place. Everyone knew about her napping place in the sacristy, and most of the mice knew, too, that she slept in her night nest under the organ pedal. But no one knew of this secret place, behind the breaker panel, where she hoarded small treasures. Carefully she stowed the green gumdrop there, rearranging the pile of gold threads—she had unraveled them, one by one, from Father Murphy's vestments; she was *so* attracted to gold—and a red satin ribbon that had come loose from a prayer book.

Then she hurried away, because she had work to do. There was so little time, and so many mice! But they had trained for this. She would start by announcing the biblical word and having it passed on. Oddly, it seemed to go well with that other word: *exterminator*.

Hildegarde took a deep breath. Then, loudly, she made the announcement: "EXODUS!"

Dutifully, because they had been taught the procedure, the mice passed the word along, calling to one another, so that the message made its way throughout the interior of the church walls.

"Exodus! Pass it on!" Vivian squeaked to her adolescent children, and shooed them off to be messengers.

"Exodus! Pass it on!" Jeremiah called through a furnace duct. In seven different locations, other mice heard it and repeated it so that the news went from mouse to mouse to mouse until each one, all but the smallest ones, knew, and knew what it meant. They all prepared to flee. They were going Outdoors.

∽

Monday night was spent organizing, collecting food, hiding evidence of their existence, and instructing the little ones, who were caught up in the excitement but didn't know why.

"What's *exodus*?" the small mouse named Harvey kept asking. He was an annoying little fellow with a very whiny voice. "What's *exodus*? What's *exodus*?" When his mother, busy with other things, didn't reply, he scampered about and bothered everyone else. Finally someone told him to go find Ignatious.

"Ask Ignatious," they said. "He'll explain."

Ignatious was very old, but new to Saint Bartholemew's. He had lived for a long time at the university library, and had become a church mouse quite by accident when he had foolishly crawled into the pocket of an overcoat that was draped across a chair during a lecture. He had fallen asleep there. Next thing he knew, the overcoat, and its owner, Father Murphy, transported him to Saint Bartholemew's and he had been there now for several months.

It wasn't much different from the library, actually. Pocket crumbs to eat still, and he had made himself a nice nest from some shredded hymnal pages. He wasn't fond of crowds and tended not to attend meetings (on the night Hildegarde had gathered the mouse congregation in Father Murphy's office, he had stayed behind, eaten some small tobacco flecks that he'd been saving, and gone to sleep), but he understood what was happening now and was preparing, like the others, to leave.

Harvey, the little whiny mouse, sought him out and pulled at his tail to get his attention. There were few things Ignatious hated more than having his tail yanked. He turned irritably and said, "What?"

"They told me to ask you what *exodus* means." Harvey folded his paws politely and looked up with big eyes.

"*Departure,*" Ignatious replied. "It's Greek." Actually, he could forgive a tail yank if someone was genuinely seeking knowledge. And he remembered Greek fondly, from the university library. He had nibbled quite a bit of Greek. "An ancient language."

"Greek?" Harvey giggled, and said it several times. "Greek? Greek?" It was so close to *squeak* that it amused him. Ignatious gave him a meaningful dark look and he subsided.

"It means 'the departure of large numbers.'"

"Of mice?"

"In this case, mice."

"Why?"

Ignatious sighed. He knew that once a young one started with *why* there would be many *whys* to follow. "Because we're in danger. We have to escape."

"To where?"

"Outdoors."

Harvey squealed nervously. "*Outdoors?*"

Ignatious held up one paw in a STOP gesture because he could see that Harvey was about to ask *why* again. Ignatious liked imparting knowledge, but he found a litany of *whys* annoying.

"Go," he said. "Stay with your mother and siblings. If you run off by yourself, you might never find your way back here. I myself made a foolish mistake once in leaving the university library, and . . ." He stopped himself. Too long a story. Not of interest to young ones.

"Oh, we're coming back?" Harvey asked.

"Of course. When the danger is past. Now GO!"

So Harvey scampered off to find his mother, chattering away, telling everyone what he had learned—"It means 'departure'! We're going away in a large group! To Outdoors! We're escaping danger! We'll be coming back! It's Greek! Greek's an ancient language!"—until finally someone swatted him on his rear and told him to shut up.

They all slept on Tuesday, all day, preparing themselves for what lay ahead.

Then it was Tuesday night and time to go. They left under cover of darkness, led by Hildegarde, with Frederick and Jeremiah dashing along the side of the procession, back and forth, keeping everyone in order and silent. No singing allowed. Mothers helped their children. Even Harvey was quiet and wide-eyed. Then, silently, they flattened themselves and more than two hundred mice squeezed under the heavy wooden front door of Saint Bartholemew's, out into the night, into Outdoors.

CHAPTER 7

Yikes! Outdoors!

When he realized why the church mice were all jumping about and giggling, Roderick explained. "It's grass," he told them. "It's called grass."

Almost none of them had ever seen, or felt, grass before. It tickled as they made their way through it in the night.

"Is this Outdoors?" Harvey squealed. "Is this what Outdoors is like?" He dashed about in the grass.

"Yes. Shhh. Come this way!" Hildegarde called. "To the churchyard cemetery!"

"This is quite an ordinary grass," Ignatious muttered, as he strode along, talking to anyone who was listening. "The correct name is *monocotyledonous graminoids*, by the way. That's Latin. I spent quite a bit of time in the botany section of the university library. Nibbled quite a few books about grasses. There are many varieties. There are some amazing ornamental grasses, for example. And on a golf green, the quality of the grass is very important. A golfer . . ."

No one was paying any attention to Ignatious. He talked on and on, but they had reached the little cemetery now and all of the church mice had spread out. They rushed around, looking for the best places to create their nests. Here and there they stopped to nibble on a flower or two. But Hildegarde was reminding them that they had to find a nicely hidden place.

"When you've found your spot, settle in and get comfy. Then before it turns light, I'll call a meeting and make a few announcements," she said.

"I'm going over there, to the base of that statue," she confided quietly to Roderick, and pointed. "Join me if you wish. I see some nice mossy crevices."

Roderick was flattered. Normally Hildegarde remained aloof. But of course this was not an ordinary time. Each of the mice felt a little insecure in such unknown territory. But at least they felt safer here than in the church. They would hide in the cemetery during the visit tomorrow of the Great X—and perhaps they would have to stay out here one more day, because a Great X sometimes sprayed poisonous fumes and they would have to wait for those to subside—but then probably Friday night, again under cover of darkness, they would make their way back into Saint Bartholemew's, just in time to prepare for the next dangerous time: the Blessing of the Animals.

Hildegarde and Roderick, working together, patted the moss at the base of the stone statue into a soft bed, concealed by a flowering bush of some kind. All around them, throughout the cemetery, they could hear small squeaks and chitters as the other church mice prepared their own spots.

"Hi!" The talkative little one, Harvey, suddenly appeared, parting the leaves of the bushes with his paws. "You got a good bed? We do! My mom found some old dead leaves! What's your statue? Can you read it? I can't read. But see there? It's got words on it!" He pointed upward. "What's it say?"

"Shhh." Hildegarde squinted up through the darkness. "It says 'Samuel Carstairs, Patriot. R.I.P.' That means 'rest in peace.'"

"And you should do that, Harvey," Roderick added. "Your mother will be wondering where you are. Go get some rest. Every young mouse should—"

"Oh, hush, Roderick," Hildegarde said. "Let him run around a bit when it's dark. He'll have to sleep all day. Harvey?"

"What?" the young mouse asked.

"Would you make the rounds and tell everyone to gather in the center of the cemetery, by the fountain? I'm going to give instructions and make some announcements."

"Do I have to?" Harvey whined. "I wanted to play with—"

"Yes. You have to. Stop that whining."

Harvey's tail, which had been twitching, sank and dragged on the ground as he trotted away. But she could hear him delivering the message, and after a few moments she could hear the rustling in the grass as all of her large tribe began to gather by the fountain.

Drat. Hildegarde could see, as she approached the fountain, that Lucretia had already scampered up its concrete side and assumed an authoritative pose, as if *she* were the one in charge. *Well.* She'd put a quick end to *that.*

"Thank you for holding my place, Lucretia," she said. "You may get down now."

Lucretia, sulking, moved off the fountain rim.

"And clean your tail when you get a chance, please," Hildegarde called after her. "There are bits of dried grass clinging to it."

That was mean, Hildegarde thought guiltily. But she did loathe Lucretia.

She turned and looked down at the crowd of mice. "We're fortunate that the water in the fountain has been turned off for the winter," she said. "Otherwise you'd never hear me."

Ignatious, in the front row, cleared his throat loudly. "It's quite an ordinary fountain," he said in his loudest voice. "Nothing like what you might find in Italy. When I lived at the—"

"That's enough, Ignatious," Hildegarde said sternly.

He harrumphed and became quiet, though he muttered something about the thirteenth-century fountain in Perugia.

Hildegarde ignored him and continued. "I know most of you have never been Outdoors before. We are not, after all, field mice!"

The audience tittered. *Field mice! Of course they weren't field mice!*

"And we will not be here long. Probably two days. But I myself have traveled a bit from time to time, and have learned to appreciate some of the dangers of the Outdoors. So I want to alert you.

"There are things to enjoy, of course. The grass is fun. And there are still some tasty flowers, in the fall.

"Do not nibble rhododendron leaves! Mothers, warn your mouse-lets! Rhododendron leaves are poi-sonous!"

Ignatious looked up. "From the Greek," he said. "*Rhodos—rose;* and *dendron—tree.*"

"Thank you, Ignatious."

"When I—"

"We know, Ignatious. You nibbled a lot of Greek at the university library."

He nodded with satisfaction. Hildegarde resumed her speech.

"Stay hidden in daytime. You're accustomed to that. And we're fortunate that they are no longer mow-ing the lawn. They stop mowing in mid-September, so our timing is perfect. A mowing machine is deadly! Many, many field mice are lost to mower blades every summer."

There was a low murmur of sympathy for field mice.

"You may come out of your nests and find food after dark. Or, yes, Harvey—you young ones may play after dark. But beware of *owls!*"

"Owls?"

"What are owls?"

Hildegarde looked down. "Ignatious? Are you spry enough to jump up here? And did you nibble your way through . . . what section of the library would *owls* be?"

"Ornithology. Yes. I know a great deal about owls. Can you give me a paw?"

Hildegarde reached down and helped him, while Jeremiah gave a boost to the old mouse's rear.

Ignatious stood, finally, on the fountain rim. He whispered to Hildegarde, "Do you want the Latin?"

"No, no. Just warn them."

"Owls are nocturnal!" Ignatious said in his biggest voice. "They operate at night!"

"Oooh," said the mice.

"There are many kinds!"

"Oooh."

"They are birds of prey!"

"Oooh."

"What's *prey*?" asked a little one.

"Prey is *us*!" Ignatious said loudly.

"Ooooooh!"

Hildegarde could see the mice looking around nervously.

"They swoop down out of trees! Almost without sound! And they snatch unsuspecting mice!"

"I want to go back to Saint Bartolemew's!" wailed Harvey. "I don't like Outdoors!"

"Thanks, Ignatious," Hildegarde said. "That's warning enough. We'll all be alert, and on the lookout, now, won't we?"

She could see that many, many pairs of wide mouse eyes were looking toward the trees nervously.

"There are two hundred species of Strigiformes— that's Latin—" Ignatious began.

"Enough!" Hildegarde said, and grudgingly he hopped down from the fountain.

"The sun is starting to rise," she pointed out, and they could see that there, in the east, behind the church steeple, the sky was lightening.

Somewhere nearby, a bird twittered. "Time to get to your nests, cuddle in, get some sleep. Today the Great X will come. His truck will come right up the driveway. Do *not* jump up to look at it! Stay hidden!

"That's all for now," she said, and the mice applauded with their soft little paws, then scampered away in every direction.

Hildegarde jumped down and headed toward her own nest at the base of the statue. Lucretia passed her, waddling along with a kind of strut. "You're such an alarmist, Hildegarde," she said, looking down her

pointed nose and twitching her whiskers. "There was no need for such fear tactics!"

At that moment, from deep in the foliage of a nearby spruce tree, came a throaty repeated hoot. *Hoo. Hoo. Hoo.*

"Oh my lord!" squeaked Lucretia in terror, and she dashed away.

Hildegarde chuckled and made her way to the mossy bed she would share tonight with Roderick.

CHAPTER 8

Ignatius Explains the Horrors

The mice slept soundly during the day, exhausted from the lengthy nighttime exodus, from the strangeness of the cemetery, and from the finding and building of nests. Outdoors was silent, except for birdsong and a breeze that rustled the leaves.

Once, in the afternoon, they were all startled awake by a sound that was new to them and sounded dangerous. Young mouselets whimpered and clutched their mothers. Ears, whiskers, and tails stiffened, and mouse noses twitched in anxiety. But it was only a human child, whistling as he rode his bicycle through the cemetery, using the gravestones as a slalom course. After a moment they all relaxed and resumed their sleep.

Hildegarde remained wakeful. She found that it was not at all pleasant, sharing a sleeping place with Roderick. He snored, and hogged the moss. Finally, restless, she crept out of the hidden nest and looked around a bit. The gravestones were old and weathered, covered with lichens; she tried nibbling one but it was slimy and tasteless. Maybe if she were *starving!* But there were yummy berries nearby, and wilted chrysanthemums on several graves. No shortage of food.

As Hildegarde crouched there at the foot of the statue, blinking her unaccustomed eyes in the daylight of Outdoors, she became aware of the sound of a vehicle approaching the church. She peeked out between some tall ferns and saw the silver van with the ominous message on its side: PEST-B-GONE. She shuddered. It was terrible, being referred to as "pest"! But she knew that's what it meant: mice. Oh, all right, probably cockroaches and carpenter ants—it meant those other things as well. They *were* pests. As were—ugh—*rats*.

But mice? Especially dear church mice, who knew the words to all the hymns and prayers? Who sang in their trusting, pious, squeaky little voices, with their eyes gazing heavenward and their tails reverently bowed? If Father Murphy only knew what treasures dwelt in his walls!

The Great X stopped its van there, at the side door of the church, and she watched as Father Murphy welcomed a man in a blue jumpsuit and invited him inside.

A rustle in the ferns startled Hildegarde, and she jumped slightly.

"Just me," said Ignatious. "Couldn't sleep. Affliction of old age: insomnia." He stretched and yawned. "Of course, in humans it can be treated with benzodiazepines such as temazepam, flunitrazepam, triazolam, flurazepam, midazolam, nitrazepam, and quazepam—"

"Oh, will you please *shut up!*" Hildegarde hissed at him.

"Sorry to offend." Ignatious did look apologetic. "It's just that I spent a lot of time in the psychopharmacology section of the univers—"

She glared at him and he fell silent.

"Look!" she said, and pointed.

Ignatious followed her pointing paw with his eyes and saw the van. "Uh-oh," he said. He squinted his aging eyes and read the title on its side. "*Pests,*" he said contemptuously. "Don't you hate that?"

"Did they ever have a Great X at the university library?" Hildegarde asked.

"Oh my, yes. Often. We lost huge numbers. Once, in the cafeteria, well . . . " He stopped talking and took a deep, mournful breath.

Hildegarde patted his back. "It's all right. Don't talk about it. I've been through it. I know what it's like."

They sat silently for a moment. Then she said to him, "I don't suppose they celebrated the Feast of Saint Francis at the university."

Ignatious shook his head. "No. I've studied the saints, though. Actually, I know quite a bit about saints. Saint Ambrose, Saint Andrew, Saint Anthony—as you can see, I'm going alphabetically here—" Then he fell silent, seeing her face.

"I'm a saint," he couldn't resist adding.

"I mean, my name is. Saint Ignatious. If I'd gotten to the *Is* you would have— "

"*Too much information,*" Hildegarde said curtly.

He stopped talking and they stared at each other.

"What do you know about cats? Have you studied cats?" Hildegarde asked him suddenly.

Ignatious shuddered. "Oh, no. I've always avoided anything in that category. Makes me squeamish. Actually, I had a good friend once, at the university library. Leonard. Sweet guy. He lived in the audio section. Nibbled at the edges of opera albums, mostly. But then one day he wandered out for a breath of fresh air, innocent as you please, and there, lying right there in the sun, was a large yellow cat, and faster than you can imagine, well . . . " He gulped. "Oh, sorry!" he said, and began to cry, wiping his eyes with a wrinkled paw.

Hildegarde patted him gently. "I know, I know. We've all experienced it," she said. They sat together silently for a moment.

There was a noise from the church. They peered again through the ferns and saw the uniformed man come out to his van. He entered it and then emerged, carrying equipment, and reentered the side door of Saint Bartholemew's.

"Traps," Ignatious said, knowingly.

"We can deal with those. I sprang two traps in the kitchen just last Sunday," Hildegarde said.

"Was that you? I overheard Lucretia say that she was the one who disarmed those traps."

"*Lucretia!*" Hildegarde drew herself up. Her whiskers quivered in outrage. "What a liar!"

Ignatious rolled his eyes. "She's campaigning, you know, to oust you and be Mouse Mistress."

Hildegarde was so angry that she couldn't speak.

"Calm down. I want to tell you something about the special traps he just carried in there. And it's something that Lucretia won't have any knowledge of. I've made quite a study of traps, you know. Back when I was at the univers—"

Hildegarde shot him her silencing glare.

"Sorry," Ignatious said. "But pull yourself together and listen."

"I'm listening. You said 'special traps'?"

Ignatious nodded. "Yes. This is horrible. Heinous, actually."

"Describe it."

"There is no spring. No nasty little piece of metal to bop you on the head. And no bait."

"No cheese?"

"*Nada.* That's Spanish, incidentally. Means 'nothing.'"

She ignored that. "How do they work, then?"

"Nice scent to them. A little rectangle of cardboard with a very enticing smell. The Great X simply sets them about in all the obvious places. Closets. Kitchen sink. Trash cans. You know: all of our usual foraging spots."

"But no cheese. You said no cheese."

"No, but the smell lures mice. I know. I've smelled it. *Terribly* tempting. So the unsuspecting mouse goes close. It doesn't look like a trap. Simply a piece of cardboard, after all."

Hildegarde shuddered. She could tell something awful was going to be described. "What happens?" she asked.

"It's covered with glue."

"*Glue?*"

Ignatious nodded solemnly. "So the mouse leans forward to sniff or nibble—you know how we do. Or reaches out with a paw."

Hildegarde cringed. *How utterly cruel!* "And gets stuck," she said.

He nodded. "Dies there. Starves."

Hildegarde couldn't speak. She was horrified.

"I saw something funny once," Ignatious said, trying to cheer her. "The janitor at the university library? He reached for his vacuum cleaner, and one of those traps was stuck under it."

Hildegarde frowned. "Nothing funny about that."

"So the janitor tried to pry it off with his foot. And his foot got stuck. So there he was, attached to his own vacuum cleaner! He had to clump down the hall, dragging all the equipment, to find someone to help him."

She smiled slightly at the thought. But *still*. It was very cruel.

"Look! There he goes!" Ignatious pointed. The

exterminator came out and tossed his bag into the back of the van. Then he got in. After a moment they watched him drive away from the church.

"So that's it? Gluey traps?" Hildegarde asked.

"No. He will have put poison around as well. There are many kinds of rodent poison—sorry to use the word *rodent—brodifacoum, zinc phosphide, difethialone—*"

"Oh, stop!" Hildegarde put her little paws over her ears. "I'd almost rather live Outdoors," she said with a sigh.

Ignatious shook his head. "It's worse out here," he said. "Much more dangerous. We didn't even tell them about *hawks.* And of course, winter's coming soon. You know what that means."

"I know. We need to be near the furnace." Hildegarde turned and parted the ferns to reveal her sleeping nest. Oh, lord—Roderick was still snoring! "Well, I'm going to lie down for a while. I'll try to figure out some survival methods to put into place for our return."

"If you don't, Lucretia will. Take my word for it."

"Thanks, Ignatious." Hildegarde plodded away.

He called after her. "And then cats! On Sunday: cats!"

As if she weren't already aware of it! Hildegarde waved one paw at him and went to lie down. She had a headache all of a sudden.

CHAPTER 9

Brave Volunteers Needed!

Two days passed. There were a few squabbles, and one crisis when several of Millicent's mouselets got lost and squealed loudly until they were located and returned to her, but on the whole it was an uneventful time. Hildegarde even noted with satisfaction that several friendships had been formed with some field mice who were already residents of the cemetery. Field mice were a lesser species, of course—not very smart and with unappealingly small ears. But she thought that it was quite benevolent and generous of her clan to befriend them. It crossed her mind that perhaps they could plan, at Christmastime, to distribute small gifts somehow to the needy but worthy population of field mice.

But mostly, her mind was on their return to Saint Bartholemew's. It was Friday evening, October second, and they had been in the cemetery long enough. She was planning to speak from the fountain once again, to give directions for the reentry that night. But she was very nervous.

"I was wondering, Hildegarde, if you would like . . ."

The voice startled her, and she looked up from her troubled thoughts. Oh, good lord: *Lucretia.*

"If I would like *what?*" she asked in a tense voice.

"Perhaps you'd like me to take over, make a speech, give instructions? You seem somewhat uncertain." Lucretia had a sly, malevolent look.

Hildegarde stared at her coldly. "I am never uncertain," she replied. "And at the moment, I am very certain that I would like you to return to your nest and wait there until I give the signal to gather."

Lucretia smirked. "Your wish is my command, Mouse Mistress," she said sarcastically. Then she turned and flounced away, her tail contemptuously erect.

⁓

"Ignatious," Hildegarde said, "I really don't know quite what to tell them. There will be such dangers to face. We can describe the poison, assuming it will be there—"

"It will be there. We can be sure of it."

"And order them to eat nothing at all but their regular fare. Cookie crumbs, pizza crust, wedding cake remains, prayer book bindings . . ."

"Candles and crayons."

"Oh, lord, yes—some of them like that waxy stuff."

"Splenda packets. Those are safe."

"And gumdrops," Hildegarde added, "though I think I'm the only one who knows where he hides them."

"I sometimes eat soap," Ignatious confessed, blushing.

"You do?" She looked at him in surprise.

He nodded. "It makes me burp bubbles," he said, with an embarrassed laugh.

"Well, soap's safe, at least. Shall I just tell them *absolutely nothing unfamiliar, no matter how tempting?*"

"Yes. And mothers must keep an eye on their mouselets. Supervise their eating."

"All right. I'll give that order. But what on earth are we to do about the glue traps, Ignatious? If the Great X has used those? In the dark, when the church mice are scurrying, thinking about food—"

"I shudder to think of it, Hildegarde."

"I can just hear the cries, Ignatious! All of my population, stuck, their little paws glued—"

"Sometimes," he said ominously, "mice lean down to sniff, and then their *nose* becomes glued!"

Hildegarde shuddered. "How do they breathe, then?"

"That's the *point*, Hildegarde. They can't."

She gasped in horror.

"There is a way of getting them loose, once they're trapped," Ignatious said. "But it's very, very difficult and time-consuming. We could perhaps manage to release *one*—but if dozens are caught, well . . ."

She sighed, and glanced at the sky. The moon had risen. "I have to go speak to them, Ignatious. They must prepare. I'll just have to—"

She was interrupted by a noisy rustle in the nearby shrubbery. Roderick pushed his way through, dragging something white. Behind him scampered Harvey, whining, as usual. "Nobody told me I couldn't! I wasn't doing anything wrong! Just looking for food!"

"Shhh." Hildegarde ordered the little mouse to be quiet. "What's this, Roderick?"

Roderick dropped what he'd been carrying clenched in his big teeth. Then he huffed and puffed, catching his breath, and finally turned to the to sulking little mouse beside him. "I'm not mad at you, Harvey! Stop fussing!"

He looked at Hildegarde and Ignatious. "Harvey here noticed that the sexton put the trash out for tomorrow's collection—"

"Yes, it's Friday. He always puts it out on Friday evenings."

"So Harvey scampered over to check on it, and—"

Harvey wiggled, waved his tail, and squeaked, "I know you told us not to leave the cemetery! But I just went for a *minute!* You know, sometimes there's good stuff in the trash! And I was going to share! I promise I was going to share!"

"Hush, Harvey, we're not upset with you," Hildegarde said impatiently. "What did he find, Roderick?"

Roderick dragged the torn paper—apparently Harvey had already shredded one corner—over to where she and Ignatious were crouched side by side. "The light's terrible," he said, "but can you read it?"

Hildegarde squinted at the paper. Mouse vision

was poor; they relied on noses and ears, mostly. She went closer and said, "Move aside, Roderick. You're blocking the moonlight." Dutifully Roderick backed up so that the full light of the risen moon illuminated the paper.

"Pest-B-Gone," she read aloud, and made a face.

Ignatious came to stand beside her and looked down as well at the paper. "Invoice," he read.

"What's *invoice*?" asked Harvey. "I don't know what *invoice* means! In voice? Is it about singing? I'm pretty good at singing! Listen!" He warbled briefly, *"Rock of ages, cleft for me, let me hide myself in theeeee . . .* ⸺

"Am I in voice? Huh? Huh?"

"Quiet, Harvey. It just means 'bill.' It's what Father Murphy had to pay the Great X." Ignatious looked at the amount written near the bottom of the page, after "total." "Yikes!" he said in astonishment. "It was a lot!"

Hildegarde was leaning forward over the paper. "We don't care what he paid. They collect that offering every Sunday. They're rich. But look here, Ignatious!

Here's the information we needed!" With one paw she pointed to the lines of text above the total amount.

"Good," Ignatious said. "He's listed the kind of poison. I know what that looks like. So we can give specific instructions about what not to nibble. But what's that written lower down? I have difficulty seeing even in the best light. Getting old! Can you read that, Hildegarde?"

"Yes. It's what we feared. He calls them 'glue boards,'" she said.

"*Glue boards?* What're *glue boards?* Like snow boards? Like skateboards? I know what those are!" Harvey arranged his rear paws as if he were on a skateboard, and stood erect, pretending to balance with his front paws. "Look! Watch me! Kickflip! A one-eighty ollie! I'm really cool!"

"STOP IT!" Hildegarde ordered him angrily.

Harvey retreated, sulking, into the bushes.

The adults ignored him. "Read the rest, about the glue boards," Ignatious said in a worried voice.

"It doesn't say anything else. Just the number, and the price."

"What number?" asked Roderick. "How many?"

Hildegarde peered at the paper again. "Fifty-two," she told them.

Ignatious gave an *oof* sound, as if he'd been punched in the belly. "Fifty-two glue boards!" he said gloomily. "How on earth can we deal with that?"

Hildegarde had risen to stand on her back legs. Her tail steadied her. She was silent for a moment, in that commanding position. Then she said to Ignatious and Roderick (but not to Harvey, who had scampered off through the foliage, doing fake skateboard moves), "I have an idea. I think I know exactly what to do."

～

Hildegarde gave instructions to Ignatious and Roderick in a firm, decisive voice. "Spread the word," she said. "Immediately! I want fifty-two volunteers. I need the bravest and strongest among us. Line them up right here. As soon as possible. There is no time to lose!"

"Must they all be male?" Roderick asked. "There's that very strong pair of females: Trina and Jean. They're always doing pushups."

"They'd be perfect. Male, female, doesn't matter. Trina and Jean will be fine. Strong! And brave! That's what we want.

"Get going! We don't have much time!" She shooed Ignatious and Roderick off on their mission.

Within ten minutes, fifty-two strong, brave mice—including Trina, Jean, and several other females—had lined up to await instructions from Hildegarde. She moved among them, explaining, gesturing, describing, encouraging.

"Could we help, Hildegarde?" Roderick asked. "Ignatious and I . . . I know we're not young. Maybe not strong! But we're brave! Aren't we, Ignatious?" He looked over at the elderly, scholarly mouse.

Ignatious cleared his throat self-consciously. "Well, I try to be, of course. I do enjoy *reading* about great bravery. Goodness, once in the university library, I nibbled at the edges of a list of Congressional Medal of Honor winners, and I remember thinking, *What if I found myself . . ."* His voice trailed off. Then he said in a soft voice, "No. I'm not brave. Sorry."

"You're wise, Ignatious. That's important, too," Hildegarde said, to comfort him, for he looked quite embarrassed and sad. "And you, Roderick? I need you here with me and Ignatious. We must count the numbers who return."

"Who return?" Roderick asked. "You mean—?"

"That's right. We may lose some brave souls tonight." She turned to the crowd of waiting mice. "Volunteers?"

Fifty-two enthusiastic squeaks responded to her. "It's time," she told them. "You all have your instructions. Do your best! Do your duty! Our prayers are with you! Now go!"

Moving in silence now, with no squeaks, no farewells, the fifty-two brave mice turned and marched in line toward Saint Bartholemew's.

CHAPTER 10

One Mouse Is Missing!

An hour passed. Then two. The cemetery was silent except for small squeaks of conversation here and there. Most of the church mice were unaware of the mission. They were simply waiting for the meeting that Hildegarde was to call, waiting to hear final instructions before their return to the church where they had lived all their lives. They chatted among themselves, recounting what they had done during their two-day vacation in the Outdoors. There had been some close calls. One mouse had barely escaped the talons of a swooping hawk; another had encountered a snake and scampered quickly away. A third had been munching on a bouquet of asters when a woman appeared quite unexpectedly with a watering can and doused him while he cowered, hidden only by a leaf. One by one they described their adventures and praised each other's outdoor courage.

But in the mossy crevice at the base of the statue, Hildegarde, Roderick, and Ignatious waited silently, with increasing apprehension. They had no way to know the time, but they watched clouds cross the moon, and the shadows lengthened around them. Not far off, an owl called. But they ignored it; an owl was nothing to them now. They had far larger concerns.

"What if *none* of them returns safely?" Roderick whispered at last.

"Some will, surely. We knew some might perish. That was the risk. But certainly some will get back here." Hildegarde tried to reassure him, though she was herself very frightened. She had been Mouse Mistress for a long time. But never before had she had to send some of her best, most valued mice into a life-threatening situation.

"Want me to go look?" Ignatious asked. "I could just go to the cemetery edge and see if there's any sign of them."

Hildegarde sighed. "No, the others will see you and start asking questions. We'll just stay here. Wait! What's that sound?" She stood on tiptoe and parted the ferns. Through the dark of the cloudy night, she squinted and could see shrubbery moving. She could see a familiar-looking ear. Her nose and tail both twitched. "Marvin?" she whispered loudly. Then she turned to the others. "I think it's Marvin!"

Indeed it was he. Marvin had been one of the fifty-two volunteers. Now he stumbled forward, panting, and collapsed in the little mossy glade. He looked completely exhausted. But his whiskers were vibrating triumphantly. "We did it!" he whispered.

"All fifty-two? Are you all safe?" Hildegarde's heart was beating rapidly.

"Not sure," he told her. "I finished first and there wasn't time to check on everyone. But most were right behind me, I know. Listen!"

They could hear the approaching mice now, and could tell from the stumbling sound of the small paws that they were no longer marching warriors. They were spent. Depleted. Breathing hard. Some even whimpering. But one after another they appeared and reported in. In a few minutes the area at the base of the statue was crowded with sprawled, panting church mice.

"Count them!" Hildegarde instructed Ignatious and Roderick.

"One, two, three . . ." She could hear them muttering the numbers as they moved among the heaps of heavy-breathing mice. "Twenty-nine, thirty . . ."

Finally they came back to her. "Fifty-one," Ignatious reported. "Maybe I counted wrong," he added, uncertainly. "I'm getting old."

Then Roderick returned, looking sad. "Fifty-one," he said. "I counted twice. I'm sorry."

"Who's missing?" Hildegarde felt she must ask, though she didn't want to hear the answer.

"Trina," they said together.

Oh, no! It couldn't be! Brave, strong Trina!

Hildegarde leapt to her feet and strode out among the recovering mice. "Who saw Trina last? Where was she?" she demanded.

Many didn't know. "It was so confusing in there! I couldn't tell one mouse from another!" one said. "So dangerous!" added another. "And dark!" several murmured.

"Jean?" Hildegarde asked. "Where's Jean?"

"She's over here," someone called. She followed the voice. Mice pointed with their paws, and she found Jean huddled on the edge of the crowd, weeping.

"Did you see her caught in a glue trap?" Hildegarde asked Jean. She was remembering that Ignatious said there was a way—a difficult way—to rescue one mouse from a glue trap. He had even described the method to her. It sounded awful.

Jean shook her head. "No. She was so careful! She didn't get caught in a trap."

"Where did you see her last, then?"

"She was right behind me. We were all finished, and we were headed out to return here, but—" She lowered her head and sobbed slightly.

"But what?"

"She went back! She said she had remembered one important thing we should do! And before I could stop her, she scurried back! I thought she'd catch up, but . . ." Jean looked up and peered around the group in the darkness. "She didn't make it, did she?"

"She hasn't made it *yet*, that's all!" Hildegarde patted Jean on the head. "Listen, all of you!" she called. Regaining their strength gradually, the mice looked up toward her.

"We have several hours of night left," she told them. "I'm going to look for Trina. If the sky begins to lighten—"

"Yes?" they asked.

"That's the time that all of the mice must move back into Saint Bartholemew's. If I'm not back, then . . ." She looked over at her two friends. "Roderick and Ignatious will call for the gathering and give instructions. Then they'll lead you back in."

"Excuse me?" A haughty voice came from the nearby ferns. "I believe I'll be the one to do that!"

"Don't count on it, Lucretia!" Hildegarde told her.

Then she dashed as fast as she could to the church, to find and perhaps rescue Trina.

∽

After wriggling in under the door and entering the narthex, Hildegarde paused and listened. No sound. "Trina?" she called, in as loud a squeak as she could manage.

Nothing.

She tiptoed forward, listening. Down the center aisle of the nave. There would be no traps there, no poison. This was the place where the congregation walked, the humans, looking for their seats each Sunday morning.

Silence.

The traps would be elsewhere, she knew, for the Great X chose carefully the places where mice (pests! rodents!) would be. There would be glue traps in all the obvious places: under the sink, in the sexton's closet, oh, all the rest of their favorite haunts. Hildegarde sighed. There was so little time left. She must find Trina, likely stuck, glued into place (maybe

her tiny sweet mouth was glued and that's why she could give no cry for help!), and then attempt to do the rescue procedure—so very difficult!—that Ignatious had described.

But where to look first? She scampered down the aisle, turned right at the chancel, and hurried through the south transept. Then, from the dark hallway, she heard, suddenly, a small noise from Father Murphy's office. She froze. Surely the priest would not be here, in the middle of the night!

The sound came again. A small huffing of breath, then a click. Hildegarde scurried to the office door and found it slightly ajar. She peeked inside. There was the telephone book, on top of the desk. She could see it in the moonlight. The framed photograph of Father Murphy's mother. The stacked magazines.

Click. "There! Got it!" squeaked a tiny voice. She recognized it, with enormous relief, as Trina's.

"Trina?" she called.

"Over here!" Trina called back. "Is that you, Hildegarde? What are you doing here? I'm on the first shelf, by the crossword puzzle book!"

Hildegarde remembered that book. Father Murphy often paused between appointments and worked on a puzzle. Quickly she scurried across the carpeting and made her way up, clinging to the draperies, to the shelf, where she found Trina tugging at a small plastic box.

"What on earth are you doing? We're all frantic about you!"

"They left things a bit of a mess in here," Trina explained. "Of course it was awfully hard, and there was so little time. Jeremiah got the card box open"— she gestured to the box, the lid to which she had just clicked into place—"and he gave out the cards. Fifty-two, just like you said. He saved one for himself, of course. I got the queen of diamonds," she added.

"Then we all set off, each with our card. And it worked! Just like you predicted! Such a clever idea, Hildegarde! Of course that's why you're Mouse Mistress! No one else could possibly have thought of it!

"Here, we can jump down now," Trina said. "I'm through in here."

"Through with *what*?"

"Just as we were leaving, after such a successful mission," she explained, "I remembered something. I remembered that we had left Father Murphy's card box open, there on the table, with all the cards gone! You know how tidy he is. He would have noticed, first thing! And it was so important to keep our presence invisible. That's why I came back, to put the lid back on the box. See? It's all tidied up and back in place. We can go now. I'm sorry I made you anxious."

"Jean was weeping."

"Oh, dear. I told her I'd be careful, but you know Jean. She's a worrier."

Together they jumped down to the floor and ran quickly across the carpet and through the crack in the door. Then they pushed it, together, with all their combined strength, until it closed.

"Could you just show me one, so I can see how it worked?" Hildegarde asked.

"Of course. On the way out. I have to tell you something, though, Hildegarde . . ."

"What's that?" They were hurrying along, side by side.

"We only found fifty-one. *Please* don't say anything to Jeremiah. He feels terrible. He had the eight of spades. But we all looked and looked, and we only found fifty-one glue boards. Finally—so much time had passed—we simply left the eight of spades in the bushes by the front door.

"Here. Come over here." Trina directed Hildegarde to the coat rack in the narthex. "Look right behind, where the little opening to the inside of the wall is."

Hildegarde knew the route well. She had entered and exited so often from that tiny hole. Now she scurried over and looked. Behind the coat rack was a glue board, a smallish rectangle, lying on the tile floor where a scurrying church mouse would have undoubtedly have stepped upon it and been caught in such a horrible way.

"Look!" said Trina merrily, and she hopped onto the glue board.

"Don't!" squealed Hildegarde, terrified.

"No, it's quite safe! Let's see . . ." Trina looked down. "It's the three of hearts. I think Malcolm had that one. See what a good job he did? Fitted it perfectly!" She danced up and down on the three of hearts, which was glued securely over the rectangular trap.

"Amazing," Hildegarde said.

"I put my queen of diamonds on one in the ladies' room, behind the sink, where the pipe comes in. It wasn't easy, Hildegarde, to get the corners straight! But I think we all did a good job."

"You did indeed! Now let's hurry back. We've got to get everyone moved back in before sunrise!"

Side by side, gleeful, the two church mice wriggled under the huge front door and scampered down the steps of Saint Bartholemew's and into the Outdoors.

A light rain was beginning to fall.

CHAPTER 11

Poor Lucretia!

Now, on Saturday night, the church mice were all back in residence once again. Most had returned to their old nests, finding them undisturbed inside the walls. The glue boards had been carefully explained to them by Hildegarde during her Departure talk, and the mice chuckled each time they skirted one. Seven of hearts, under the kitchen sink. Jack of clubs, in the sexton's closet: Harvey, mischievous, had left some droppings on that one.

There was even a five of spades under the organ console, very close to Hildegarde's sleeping nest. She

pushed it aside with a laugh. Oh, sometime the Great X would return, she knew, summoned again by Father Murphy, who would eventually miss his solitaire cards, and by the sexton, who would be mystified as he found them here and there throughout the church.

The Exterminator page of the telephone book, though, had been carefully eaten. Jeremiah had done it all alone, a big job, but he felt that he needed to atone for not being able to find the fifty-second glue board. His eight of spades was still in the bushes by the church steps, wet now, for it had been drizzling for twenty-four hours.

Hildegarde busied herself throughout the night, reminding the mice that tomorrow was the Feast of Saint Francis, the celebration that ordinarily they watched through the windows and peepholes. But the windy rain had increased during the night, and as the first light came, she made the rounds again, warning them all.

"It will be indoors," she said briskly, trying not to alarm them too much. It had been some years since it had rained on the day of the Blessing of the Animals.

Most of the mice were too young to know anything but the outdoor ceremony and its amusing confusion. Ignatious was old enough, but he had been living at the university library then. So even he, with all his knowledge, was unaware of the impending danger.

"Stay hidden," she admonished them over and over. "Deeply hidden."

"I wanna watch!" Harvey whined. "Why can't we watch?"

"There will be cats. Many cats."

"I'm not scared of cats! I could bite cats!" Harvey bared his big crooked front teeth.

Hildegarde shook him. "Listen to me! Cats are our *worst* enemy! You must *fear* cats! And you must watch only from the most hidden and inaccessible places. Inside an air vent. Top of an organ pipe, if you can climb up there—they're slippery."

"In a cushion? I could be in a cushion!" Harvey suggested.

"No! Cats have terrible claws. They could rip a cushion—and you—apart in seconds!"

"Oh, darn," Harvey said, and went off sulking.

Hildegarde turned back to the assembled, nervous mice. "Find your hiding places now," she said, "because . . ." She assessed the light through the stained-glass windows. Rain made light very different, so it was hard to tell the time. " . . . it may be starting before long. Listen for the organ. When Trevor Fisoli begins to practice, you must absolutely be hidden."

Hildegarde watched as all of them, even Harvey, obediently scampered off to hide themselves. Oh, she hoped she could keep them safe! They were so dear to her! Most of them, anyway.

"Where's Lucretia?" she asked Roderick, who was by her side. "I haven't seen Lucretia this morning."

He shrugged. "Dunno. Probably up to no good."

"Well, I hope she has a hiding place planned. How about you, Roderick? Where are you headed?"

"Not sure. I was thinking about maybe under the mop in the sexton's closet. He won't be cleaning this morning."

"Well, he will be, but it'll be when the ceremony ends. He'll have to clean up after the animals. You know they lose control, often. Disgusting. Dogs especially."

"Think he'll need his mop?" Roderick asked.

"Probably. Especially if that horse comes."

"Well, I'd better find a different place, then. Where are you going, Hildegarde?"

She hesitated. She was planning to head to the sacristy, her own special, private place. She thought that she might be able to peek through the keyhole of the sacristy door and get a bit of a glimpse. Was it selfish to keep a place so private and out-of-bounds only for herself? Maybe it was. And Roderick was so very loyal, and—yes, she had to admit—sweet. So she gave in.

"Come with me, Roderick. We'll go to the sacristy. We can curl up under the surplices while Father Murphy vests himself. Then, after he leaves, we'll have the room to ourselves and I think I can figure out a way to peek at the ceremony."

"The sacristy? I'm honored, Hildegarde. Thank you!" Roderick indeed looked very grateful and affectionate. Hildegarde knew, actually, that he had a bit of a crush on her. She had always thought that they were too old for that kind of foolishness. But now? With cats about to enter the church? With dangers to face? It seemed, for the first time, important to have a special friend.

They could hear Trevor Fisoli arrive and mount the stairs to the organ loft. In a moment he would start the resounding chords that always began his practice. Hildegarde and Roderick, side by side, scampered hastily to the sacristy to hide themselves.

But when they entered the small, quiet space, they were alarmed to hear a terrible cry. It was somewhat muffled, coming from the corner near the closet where the most important chasubles, albs, and stoles were stored. Hildegarde and Roderick froze. It was clearly the cry of a mouse. A wail, a scream! Somewhere in this room a mouse—one of *her* mice, Hildegarde realized—was suffering some kind of horrible torture.

They rushed forward, pushed the bottom of the thick draperies aside, and saw the catastrophe immediately. It was Lucretia, caught by all four feet, and her tail, as well, adhered to the only uncarded glue board. *Eight of spades*, Hildegarde thought. *This one should have been the eight of spades.*

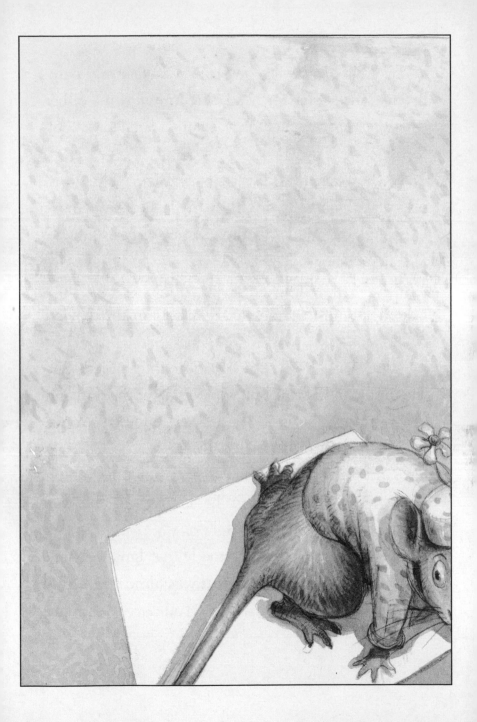

Lucretia's face was contorted with fear and pain. Even as she shook her head, screaming, some of her whiskers were caught. One was pulled out! How awful, to lose a whisker!

In the background, they heard Trevor begin to play scales. Then he ran through "Jesu, Joy of Man's Desiring," one of his favorite practice pieces.

Lucretia howled.

"Oh, what should we do? What can we do?" Roderick whimpered. He began to run in frenzied circles.

"Don't touch it!" Hildegarde commanded. She feared that in his panic he would grab at the trap and become caught himself. "Be still for a moment! You're distracting me, and I need to think."

"And Lucretia? Be quiet!" she ordered. What on earth was Lucretia doing in here, anyway? This was Hildegarde's private space!

She did remember the remedy that Ignatious had described. But my goodness! It was almost impossible. "Olive oil!" she said aloud. "You have to saturate the glued parts of the victim with olive oil, Roderick. Do we have any? Is there some in the kitchen?"

Roderick nodded. "In the pantry. But it's a big can, brand new, hasn't been opened yet."

"Could we bite through it?"

"Not tin. No."

"Unscrew the lid?"

"No. Not even the church ladies can get it open. They always call in the sexton to help. And even *he* grunts and groans."

Lucretia wailed loudly. "Help! Help me!" Hildegarde could see another whisker rip off.

"Quiet, Lucretia! You got yourself into this. You should never have been in here. I'm going to help you, but you have to keep still." *Dumb thing to say. Of course she'll keep still. All four paws are glued tight.*

Hildegrade remembered something. It might work. No way to know. But it was the only hope.

"See that shelf?" Hildegarde pointed to a high shelf on which stood a glass container decorated with silver filigree. "I have to get up there."

"Shouldn't be too hard," Roderick said. "You climb things higher than that all the time. What's in that bottle?"

Hildegarde didn't answer him. She was still thinking. From the place at the foot of the drapery, Lucretia let out another wail of misery. Hildegarde ignored that. "Roderick," she said, "you must go out to the sanctuary. Has anyone arrived yet?" He peeked out the door and shook his head. They could still hear Trevor pounding away on the organ in the loft. But there were no other people in the church.

"Go bite into a cushion. Any cushion. Can you do that?"

Roderick nodded uncertainly. "I guess so. Then what? Do I have to eat a cushion? I'm not sure my digestive tract can—"

"No. Don't eat it. Pull out some stuffing and drag it back here."

"Why?"

Hildegarde looked at him impatiently. "You'll see.

We don't have much time, Roderick! Father Murphy is going to be here any second. Bring back the stuffing. I'll be up on that shelf. Go!"

Roderick scurried away.

"And you: be quiet!" Hildegarde called to Lucretia. Then she jumped to the arm of a chair, and from there to the sink counter. She eyed the distance to the shelf. It was still pretty far. She jumped next to a hook on the wall, and from there took a deep breath, then leapt to the shelf.

There! Now she was where she needed to be. Not a bad leap for an old lady, she thought.

She stood erect, held tightly with her paws to the glass bottle, and nudged at the stopper with her nose. The cork moved slightly. She nudged again. And again. *There.* It was out. It bounced once on the shelf, and fell to the carpeting.

"Roderick?" she called. He appeared in the doorway, dragging a length of gray cushion stuffing with his mouth. Still holding it, he looked up at her questioningly.

"Good!" she said. "Now I need that up here. Jump first to the arm of the chair. Don't drop the stuffing!"

He did that, and looked up at her again.

"Now to the sink. It's an easy jump."

He made it to the sink.

"Get a really good grip on the stuffing now, Roderick, because the next one's quite a leap!"

Looking nervous, Roderick rearranged the position of his teeth a bit. "Over and up to that hook," she directed him. "You can do it! I did!"

From the trap on the floor came a small voice. "I'm praying for you!" Lucretia called.

Well, that's a first, thought Hildegarde. "Go, Roderick!"

He took a deep breath, around the stuffing, and jumped to the hook.

"Now to the shelf!" she called to him.

He did it, and dropped the stuffing by her side.

"That was scary," he said. "And it was scary in the

sanctuary, with the organ playing! I grabbed a cushion in the first pew, and—"

"Later, Roderick. Tell me later. No time now. I need you to wrap my tail with the stuffing."

He looked very puzzled. But he followed Hildegarde's directions and carefully wound the gray fluffy material around her tail as she held it out to him.

"Good. Ignatious said to use a Q-tip, but of course we don't have one. This should do. Now stand right here. I'm going to climb you."

Roderick leaned against the crystal and silver container and Hildegarde carefully climbed to his shoulders, then placed her rear paws, one by one, on the top of his head.

"Ouch!"

"Can't be helped!" she told him. "Now hold very still."

He did so, and she lifted her cotton-coated tail up, and up, then curled it and dipped it into the open top of the container.

"What's in there?" Roderick asked when she brought her tail out, dripping.

"Chrism."

"*Chrism?* What's that?" As she lowered her tail, he sniffed it. "Smells like the pine trees in the cemetery."

"It's holy oil," she told him. "Actually, olive oil scented with balsam. Help me down now."

Getting down was slightly easier than getting up had been, even though her tail was heavy with wadded, oily cotton stuffing. Hildegarde went first. Holding her tail up so as not to smear the carpeting, she scurried over to where Lucretia waited.

"Hold my tail so it doesn't touch the glue, Roderick, and then squeeze," she directed him.

Little by little they dabbed the oil on Lucretia's glued parts while she whimpered. Several whiskers were hopelessly lost. But carefully, one by one, they were able to extricate her legs. Finally, only her tail was still stuck to the trap. With one last squeeze of the remaining oil, they moistened it, then tugged. Lucretia howled in pain, but the tail came loose at last and she toppled onto the carpet. Her fur was torn and mottled, and one paw was bleeding. She was weak, and weeping. But she was free. "Thank you," she gasped.

"Go and hide quickly," Hildegarde told her. "The service will be starting soon. Roderick and I will clean up in here."

Lucretia turned and limped heavily toward the door. Then she looked back with gratitude. "Hildegarde," she said, "you're a saint."

CHAPTER 12

The Blessing of the Animals

Ignatious appeared at the slightly opened door. "The pews are filling up! And the procession's lining up outside!" he said. "Dripping wet!"

They could hear Father Murphy approaching the sacristy. "Hide in here with us, Ignatious!" Hildegarde suggested quickly. "Get behind the draperies, and be quiet while he puts his vestments on. Then we can go peek out and watch, after he leaves."

Ignatious scurried across the room and crouched behind the heavy draperies with Hildegarde and Roderick. "Oh my lord, what's that?" he whispered, pointing to the glue trap which they had pushed against the wall. "And whose fur is on it?"

"Shhh. Lucretia's. But she's all right. We got her out."

"Duck!" said Roderick. "Here he comes."

Father Murphy entered and looked around. They held their breath. Hildegarde watched his black shoes move across the carpet, and then his hand reach down and pick up the cork that was lying on the floor. There was no way that she and Roderick could have returned the cork to the shelf.

"Oops! Popped your cork, did you?" They heard him chuckle. The sounds indicated that he had reached for the container of holy oil and moved it to the sink counter.

Then he opened the closet, removed his hanging vestments, and clothed himself for the ceremony. He was humming. Finally he took a deep breath and left the sacristy.

They could hear Trevor play a loud chord and the congregation began to sing. *"All things bright and beautiful, all creatures great and small . . ."* After all the verses of the hymn, Father Murphy would make some announcements, as always. Then the procession of the animals would begin.

Hildegarde whispered to Ignatious, a little shyly, "She called me a saint."

"Who did?"

"Lucretia. Because I got her out of the glue trap. I used holy oil."

"Well, you *are* a saint, then! And actually, there *is* a Saint Hildegarde! Right up there among Saint Helena, Saint Honorata, Saint Hyacinth . . ."

Roderick interrupted. "What exactly is a saint, Ignatious?"

Well! As if it weren't obvious! What a downright silly question! Hildegarde sniffed and raised an eyebrow at Roderick. What an old fool! But he was so sweet.

Ignatious frowned, and thought for a moment about the question. Then he said, "Someone who is especially blessed."

They were all silent for a moment. The music had stopped. They could hear Father Murphy say a few words about the Youth Group, about a special choir rehearsal, about a potluck supper. Then he announced loudly, "If the sexton would please open the doors now? Let the Blessing of the Animals begin!"

The doors of the church opened, and a small boy wearing a yellow slicker entered, carrying a wiggling puppy. Grinning broadly, he walked down the aisle. Father Murphy began:

> *"Heavenly Father, we give thanks*
> *for the creatures of Thy creation,*
> *each unique and wonderful . . . "*

The little boy reached the chancel steps, where Father Murphy was standing. The container of holy oil was beside him on a small table. He dipped his fingers into it. The priest touched the head of the puppy, smiled when it tried to lick his fingers, and murmured, "Bless this pet." Then he went on:

> *". . . for enormous ones like the elephant*
> *and hippo,*

those that are humped like the camel,
or horned like the rhino . . . "

"That's just downright silly," Hildegarde whispered.

"Bless this pet," Father Murphy murmured, touching a bunny held up by a little girl.

"No camels here! No rhinoceros!" Hildegarde said. "What on earth is he talking about?"

"Shhh," Ignatious cautioned her.

". . . for funny monkeys, furry bunnies,
friendly dogs and cats . . . "

"Friendly? Cat? That's outrageous!" Hildegarde could barely contain herself.

But Father Murphy had now said "Bless this pet" to several cats as well as a large three-legged dog, and next was a parrot in a cage entwined with flowers. One by one the owners with their animals, each decorated with ribbons or flowers for the occasion, approached him.

*" . . . for timid birds, sleek golden fish, for the
lowly turtle and the majestic horse . . . "*

"No horse in sight," Roderick said.

"Pony coming, though," Ignatious pointed out.

Indeed, a young girl led a pony with a braided
mane down the aisle. The pony actually seemed to
bow its head as Father Murphy touched it gently and
murmured his blessing.

*". . . for jungle beasts like the lion and
leopard . . ."*

Hildegarde snorted. Lion and leopard? The idiocy! More cats. Many more cats.

> ". . . *for the awkward giraffe and the*
> *curious fawn . . . "*

Next, a turtle—there seemed to be a turtle every year. Then yet another cat, followed by a Dalmatian with a flower tucked into its collar.

And more cats still. The procession moved forward slowly.

"I cannot stand this another minute! Follow me!" Hildegarde suddenly ordered her two friends. She turned and scurried out the back door of the sacristy, then into the wall and down the tangle of wires into the basement.

Ignatious and Roderick hurried along behind her, puzzled. She jumped up to the breaker panel and reached behind it into her cache of treasured things. "Here!" she said to Ignatious and Roderick, who were waiting on the floor, looking up at her. She nudged the contents of the little collection and the things fell down to them. Hildegarde jumped down and stood upright on her hind paws. She said, "Decorate me."

"What?" Roderick said in astonishment.

"*Timid birds and sleek golden fish?* Excuse me? And no mice? They thought they could get away with ignoring mice? There's going to be a mouse in this ceremony! And I'm it!"

"But there are cats!" Roderick said nervously. "Many, many cats."

"I'll risk it. It isn't fair that he doesn't bless a mouse! I'll risk it on behalf of all of us!

"Saints do this kind of thing all the time," she added gently, as an explanation.

Ignatious had pawed though the little pile of her collected treasures. He picked up a green gumdrop and placed it carefully on Hildegarde's head.

"Tie it down," she commanded.

"Oh, dear," said Roderick. "How?" He picked up the red satin ribbon that had once been a bookmark in the Book of Common Prayer, and tossed it over the gumdrop so that both ends fell to the sides of her face, behind her ears. Then he tied a bow beneath her chin.

"There!" he said. "Very becoming!"

Ignatious agreed, with an admiring nod.

"What else?" Hildegarde asked. She couldn't look down. She had to hold her head quite carefully because of the gumdrop hat.

"Two gold threads. Quite lovely." Roderick held them up.

"Around my neck, you think?"

"Perfect," Roderick said, and draped them there. "You're gorgeous."

Hildegarde blushed, briefly. Then she said, "I'll go through the undercroft and up the steps to the narthex. I'm not too late, am I?"

They all listened. There were still footsteps moving down the aisle. "No," said Ignatious. "But better hurry!"

They followed Hildegarde as she made her way, head held high, up the steps. The final participants in the procession were just starting down the aisle: a pair of perfectly matched standard poodles, parading on either side of a woman who held a leash in each hand.

"Nobody's leaving after the blessing," Ignatious pointed out to Hildegarde in a worried voice, "except the pony—they took the pony outside. But everyone else is sitting in the pews! Birds and bunnies and dogs—and cats! Lots and lots of cats!"

"Oh, do be careful, dear," Roderick said, wringing his paws.

Hildegarde waited until the pair of poodles was halfway down the aisle. Impulsively she kissed Roderick on his cheek, just where his whiskers began. Then she took a deep breath. And solemnly, slowly, majestically, she began to walk.

No one noticed.

Father Murphy continued:

"Dear Lord, keep us mindful that we are

> *all Thy creation, that we share this earth*
> *and its bounty . . . "*

He leaned down and blessed the poodles, one at a time.

Next he picked up the container of holy oil and recorked it. Then he began to conclude the prayer:

> *". . . and that man and Thy creatures can*
> *live in peace with one another . . . "*

"Look!" called out a very little boy wearing corduroy overalls. He stood up in a pew, and with one pudgy finger pointed to the floor of the center aisle. There was a stir in the congregation. People looked where the child was indicating. Several stood. One lady said "Eeek" very softly. But most smiled.

Hildegarde continued walking at an even and reverent pace. Very carefully, so as not to disturb her gumdrop, she turned her head slowly from side to side and nodded at the members of the congregation.

A low, rumbling sound began.

Father Murphy, confused at first by the sudden murmurs from the parishioners, as well as the odd rumbling noise, looked up, then around, and finally down. Hildegarde was standing in front of him now. With a broad smile, he reached down gently and picked her up.

It was *terrifying.* To be within a human hand! Had it ever happened to a mouse before? But Hildegarde breathed deeply and fought off her fear. She had, after all, in the past few days, led a successful exodus of more than two hundred mice to Outdoors and saved them all from the Great X. She had kissed dear old Roderick for the very first time. And on top of *that,* she had rescued Lucretia, which had been not at all easy!

He was holding her high up and looking at her with amused blue eyes. Trevor Fisoli had begun to play the introductory chords to the final hymn. But no one had opened a hymnal. They were all watching Father Murphy and Hildegarde. The organ music slowed and stopped, but the rumbling noise continued.

"Did you steal that gumdrop out of my drawer?" Father Murphy asked in a suspicious voice.

"Yes," she squeaked guiltily. "I have done those things which I ought not to have done."

"And those gold threads? From my chasuble, aren't they?"

"I'm sorry," she squeaked.

He hesitated. Then he whispered, "If I leave the green gumdrops for you, will you stay out of my chocolates?"

That was easy. Chocolate always stuck to her whiskers. "Yes, I promise," she squeaked firmly.

"What is that sticky mess on your tail?" he asked her.

She gulped. "Cushion stuffing and holy oil," she squeaked. Then she corrected her terminology. "Chrism."

He looked at her for a long time.

Finally he spoke again. "There are more of you, aren't there?"

She couldn't lie to him. "Two hundred and nineteen, " she whispered. "Not counting me."

Father Murphy's eyes widened. Then he shook his head, chuckling. He touched her forehead, just below the gumdrop, with his thumb, very gently.

"Bless this mouse," he said in a loud voice to the congregation. "And all mice," he added, more quietly.

Then he placed her carefully on his shoulder. She grasped the embroidered fabric of his chasuble and pulled herself upright so that she could look out at the crowd. She felt very grand.

The muted rumble continued, and Hildegarde realized, suddenly, what it was. It was the happy purr of many cats, in unison.

"Hymn number two eighty-seven," Father Murphy announced. The organ struck a chord, and his parishioners stood and began to sing.

"For all the saints, who from their labors rest . . ."

Hildegarde didn't know the words, but she was able to join in on the chorus when the music swelled. She could tell that Trevor was using the expression pedal, just above her sleeping nest.

"Alleluia," she sang. *"Alleluia!"*

AMEN